Parenting programmes
and minority ethnic families
Experiences and outcomes

Jane Barlow, Richard Shaw and Sarah Stewart-Brown
In conjunction with REU

national
children's
bureau
making a difference

The National Children's Bureau promotes the interests and well-being of all children and young people across every aspect of their lives. NCB advocates the participation of children and young people in all matters affecting them. NCB challenges disadvantage in childhood.

NCB achieves its mission by
- ensuring the views of children and young people are listened to and taken into account at all times
- playing an active role in policy development and advocacy
- undertaking high quality research and work from an evidence based perspective
- promoting multidisciplinary, cross-agency partnerships
- identifying, developing and promoting good practice
- disseminating information to professionals, policy makers, parents and children and young people

NCB has adopted and works within the UN Convention on the Rights of the Child.

Several Councils and Fora are based at NCB and contribute significantly to the breadth of its influence. It also works in partnership with Children in Scotland and Children in Wales and other voluntary organisations concerned for children and their families.

The Joseph Rowntree Foundation has supported this project as part of its programme of research and innovative development projects, which it hopes will be of value to policy makers, practitioners and service users.

The views expressed in this book are those of the authors and not necessarily those of the National Children's Bureau, the Joseph Rowntree Foundation or the University of Oxford.

Published by the National Children's Bureau for the Joseph Rowntree Foundation.
National Children's Bureau Registered Charity number 258825. 8 Wakley Street, London EC1V 7QE.
Tel: 020 7843 6000

© University of Oxford
Published 2004

ISBN 1 904787 13 4

British Library Cataloguing in Publication Data
A catalogue record for this book is available from the British Library

Designed and typeset by Jeff Teader

Contents

Acknowledgements

We would particularly like to extend our thanks to Susan Taylor of the Joseph Rowntree Foundation for her help and support.

Thank you to the Royal College of General Practitioners for permission to reproduce the section 'Later parenting practices and attitudes' from a chapter by Jane Barlow entitled 'Parenting and Psychosocial Development: the role of General Practitioners and Primary Care' in Promoting Child Health in Primary Care (Harnden and Sheikh, 2002).

1. The importance of parenting

What is parenting?

Parenting is one of society's most 'personal and possibly most important activities' (Alvy, 1988, p.142) because it is through parenting that our 'most cherished personal, religious and cultural values are transmitted' (ibid.). Parenting does, as such, play a central role in creating and sustaining societies by developing shared identities and value systems, and through its contribution to social capital. What parents do and the way that they do it also influences many aspects of children's individual lives, particularly their social and emotional development. This is due to the fact that children's development is fostered in the context of parent–child relationships, and can play an important role in the development of childhood behaviour problems, delinquency, criminality and violence. These relationships can also have both short- and long-term effects on children's mental and physical health and on their educational achievement (see below for further discussion).

While it is possible to make some broad generalisations about 'what parenting is', there is currently little known about the perceptions and practices of 'normal' or 'successful' parents. There is some evidence about the objectives that many parents have for their children, and this suggests that while parents rarely have particular goals concerning their children's education or careers, most have 'conventional aspirations to normality and adjustment' for their children (Grimshaw and McGuire, 1998). Most parents want their children to be able to adjust to society in terms of 'having a sense of right and wrong, being happy and so on' (ibid.). While it seems likely that such aspirations are common to all parents irrespective of race or culture, parenting (including parents' socialisation) is nevertheless, influenced by cultural values (e.g. National Research Council Institute of Medicine, 2000).

Parenting and cultural values

Some of the objectives that parents have for their children are particular to their culture, and may be informed by cultural theories about what constitutes a competent and successful adult (National Research Council Institute of Medicine, 2000; Ogbu, 1981). This suggests that different cultures have unique views about what parents need to do to encourage the development of such children and adults. For example, it is suggested that European and American cultures place great value on independence, achievement, competition, personal empowerment, and individuality, and that as a result there is considerable emphasis on socialising children to be independent, competitive achievers. Similarly, it is suggested that African-American and Asian cultures, in which there has been a long history of relying on the family for survival, place greater value on interdependence (Gross, 1996), and that as a result they attach greater importance to socialising children to be cooperative, obedient, sharing, and to respect authority without question (ibid.). This has led some working within the field to conclude (Carlson and Harwood, 2003) that families belonging to these ethnic groups combine the high levels of control and forceful discipline characterised by Baumrind's 'Authoritarian' parenting (defined as parenting which is restrictive and demanding, and in which conformity is required and discipline is severe and punitive) with the warmth and responsiveness which is characterised by the 'Authoritative' style (defined as parenting which is both responsive and restrictive, but in a way which is fair, consistent and takes the needs of both children and parents into account). The term 'training parenting' has been used to describe the parenting style among Chinese parents and 'no-nonsense parenting' to describe a similar style among African-American parents (Brody and Flor, 1998 in Carlson and Harwood, 2003). These are value judgements, and it is not clear to what extent it is helpful to characterise the parenting practices of parents in different ethnic groups in this way. This can be demonstrated, for example, in relation to the issue of physical punishment. While some have argued that physical punishment is a feature of black parenting (Myers and others, 1992), thereby suggesting a cultural basis for the practice, a recent study of intragroup differences in the parenting styles of African-Americans showed that mothers who were less educated were more restrictive, and that older and better educated mothers were less likely to use physical punishment (Kelley, Sanchez-Hucles and Walker, 1993 in Schutt-Aine, 1994). These findings suggest that the use of physical discipline by black parents may be mediated by socio-economic group, rather than by 'culture'. Similarly, abusive and neglectful parenting practices are more commonly found in families living on welfare (Brown and others, 1998), and encouragement and support are more common in economically advantaged families (Hart and Ridley, 1995).

Important economic and social factors that may also influence parenting include educational status, marital status, social network support, poverty, unemployment, dissatisfaction with work, and lack of information about child development (Belsky and Vondra, 1989). Irrespective of the factors involved, the implications of a model which stresses the need to locate parenting practices within a social, cultural or personal context is that an understanding of the views of parents, and the 'theories of child competence and success' which evolve from these, are important in providing appropriate methods of parent support and education (Gross, 1996).

Defining 'good' parenting

The literature on parenting styles and practices makes clear that some approaches increase the risk of deleterious outcomes for children and can be described as unhelpful for emotional and social development (see below). There has been much less research on what constitutes optimum parenting and it has been suggested that there may not be a single optimum approach. Discussions about parenting styles are complicated by the labels attached to them. The term 'good parenting' inevitably suggests that there is also 'bad parenting' and both terms are overly simplistic as descriptions of relationships extending over half a lifetime or more. Perhaps, more importantly, it implies that there are 'good' and 'bad' parents. Such labels are unhelpful. Possibly one of the most important ways in which we learn about our role as parents is by drawing on our own experience of being parented. Within this constraint, the great majority of parents try very hard to do their best for their children often in very unpropitious circumstances. This makes them 'good parents' even if they may inadvertently be parenting in a way that is not helpful for their children.

This issue is further complicated by the fact that parenting practices may differ within different ethnic groups. If it is acknowledged that the outcomes of certain parenting practices are regarded as desirable in one cultural context and not in another, it may not be possible to define an approach to parenting which is optimal in all ethnic groups. For example, 'Authoritative Parenting' (see above) may be regarded as the optimum style by White-European researchers because it gives rise to optimal outcomes in terms of aspects of psychological development that are valued among White-European families. However, if authoritative parenting is valued because it produces highly competitive and individualistic adults, it may not provide the best chance of success in a society that values cooperation and obedience.

Furthermore, some parenting practices can have both 'good' and 'bad' outcomes. For example, it has been suggested that the valuing of interdependence in Japanese culture means that Japanese babies share beds with parents, grandparents or siblings until they are 15 years of age. This contrasts quite starkly with the practices of European/American parents who it is suggested value independence, thereby adopting independent sleeping arrangements from the first few days and weeks of an infant's life (Gross, 1996). In both societies sleeping arrangements may reflect fundamental values about child-rearing goals and interpersonal relations (Morelli and others, 1992). While recent evidence has shown that long-term co-sleeping may result in sleep patterns that indicate stress (Hunsley and Thoman, 2002), there is also evidence to show that co-sleeping in infancy may protect against poor outcomes such as Sudden Infant Death Syndrome (McKenna and others, 1995).

The parenting practices of many cultures are also changing over time. For example, the literature suggests that Chinese parenting practices have historically been influenced by Confucianism with its emphasis on parents' control, obedience, strict discipline, filial piety, respect for elders, family obligations, maintenance of harmony and negation of conflict (Lin and Fu, 1990). More recently these practices have been challenged from within Chinese culture by mental health professionals, who have begun to question traditional parent–child relationships with their emphasis on discipline and control of children (Chau and Landreth, 1997) and to advocate a greater expression of warmth and affection (Lau and others, 1990). Similarly it has been suggested that 'coercive' parenting practices such as corporal punishment may have evolved and become institutionalised in black culture in order to protect children from the harsh consequences of violating racist social taboos (e.g. Johnson and others, 1980). This is also being challenged on the grounds that 'despite some adaptive utility within dangerous inner-cities', these practices may ultimately interfere with the development of 'empowered individuals who can strive for social change and economic achievement in the modern era' (e.g. Halpern, 1990; Clark, 1983). Alternative methods of discipline are being recommended.

While it remains possible that cultural factors preclude the possibility of defining 'optimal' parenting in general, it seems likely that children have many common needs that transcend cultural differences, and that these needs may be better met by certain parenting practices than others. For example, it seems clear that parents' warmth and responsiveness are necessary for healthy psychological development, irrespective of cultural context. Similarly, recent research on attachment has pointed to the importance of 'sensitive' and 'responsive' parenting that is neither overstimulating nor understimulating in terms of meeting the needs of all infants, irrespective of race or culture (Carlson and Harwood, 2003). Indeed, it has been suggested that it is the balance between 'responsiveness' and 'demandingness' that underpins later models of 'sensitive' or 'good' parenting and in particular Baumrind's different parenting styles (ibid.). More recently it has been argued that factors such as level of coerciveness and quality of communication should be added to Baumrind's model because this would permit characterisation of a greater diversity of parenting styles (ibid.), and would include the more controlling parenting that is supposedly found among cultures that have been characterised as being 'interdependent' (ibid.). It would also permit us to think in more nuanced ways about the outcomes of different combinations of parenting practices.

Why is parenting important?

There is strong evidence pointing to the importance of parenting for later well-being. Positive proactive parenting (involving praise, encouragement, warmth and affection, clear boundaries and positive discipline) is associated with high child self-esteem and social and academic competence, and protects against antisocial behaviour and substance misuse (Baumrind, 1989, 1985; Barnes, 1984; Cohen, Richardson and Labree, 1994). Parenting practices such as harsh and inconsistent discipline, little positive involvement with the child, and poor monitoring and supervision (McCord, McCord and Howard, 1963; Loeber and Dishion, 1983; Patterson, DeBaryshe and Ramscy, 1989; Patterson, Dishion and Chamberlain, 1993) are associated with a range of poor outcomes in children including delinquency, criminality, violence and substance abuse (Baumrind, 1989, 1985; Patterson, Dishion and Chamberlain, 1993; Patterson, DeBaryshe and Ramsey, 1989). The expression of negative emotion by parents including behaviours such as shouting at and hitting children, and the expression of negative reactions to children's expression of emotion, have also been shown to predict low self-esteem and social incompetence (Eisenberg, 1998). Such children are at high risk of emotional and behavioural problems, both in the short term (Wenzlaff and Eisenberg, 1998) and long term (Eisenberg and others, 1999).

Structural equation models show that a small number of parenting practices could account for as much as 30 to 40 per cent of antisocial behaviour in children and adolescents (Patterson, Dishion and Chamberlain, 1993). Four attributes of parents' behaviour have been identified in these models – a lack of positive regard, lack of warmth, inconsistent and harsh discipline, and poor monitoring and supervision. Proactive and consistent parenting practices such as displaying a supportive presence, giving clear instructions, and limit setting, have been shown to predict the presence of fewer behaviour problems in children (Denham and others, 2000).

A high proportion of emotional and behavioural problems in childhood persist into adolescence and adulthood, and these are associated with an increased risk of poor mental health (depression, alcohol, and drug misuse) and psychosocial problems (poor work and marital outcomes, delinquency, and criminal behaviour) (e.g. Moffit and others, 1996; Rutter, 1996; Champion, Goodall and Rutter, 1995; Offord and Bennett, 1994). A recent review showed direct links between parenting and adult mental health (Stewart-Brown and others, 2002).

Parenting practices have also been shown to influence psychological health and health-related lifestyles in adolescence. 'Authoritative' parenting has, for example, been shown to be associated with an internal locus-of-control and robust self-concept (scholastic competence, social acceptance, close friendships, behavioural conduct, and global self-worth). This is in contrast to the negative effects of 'permissive' parenting (defined as parenting which is responsive and accepting, but non-restrictive) and 'authoritarian' parenting (McClun and Merrell, 1998). Positive parent–child relationships that include the use of praise, encouragement, physical affection, good communication, and time spent with parents have been shown to be protective against disruptive behaviour and misuse of substances (ibid.). A high level of 'parental nurturance' has also been shown to be protective against alcohol misuse and other 'deviant' behaviours (Barnes, 1984).

A few studies indicate that parenting can also have an impact on physical health both in adolescence and in adulthood. In one study, responses to a 'family attitude' questionnaire and 'closeness to parents' scale by adolescents predicted the development of cancer in middle age (Thomas, 1976; Thomas, Duszynski and Shaffer, 1979; Shaffer, Duszynski and Thomas, 1982). The predictive power was stronger for the more life-threatening cancers, and remained after adjustment for other cancer risk factors such as smoking and radiation exposure. A further study showed that quality of 'parents' caring', also measured in late adolescence, predicted doctor-diagnosed illness 35 years later (Russek and Schwartz, 1997a, 1997b). The risk was increased three to fourfold and was shown to be independent of family history of illness, smoking, and the subject's marital history. This study demonstrated a direct relationship between 'parents' caring' and physical health in middle age. A further longitudinal study showed that family dissension in childhood was predictive of illness in later life, even after controlling for indicators of socio-economic deprivation such as family size and economic hardship (Lundberg, 1997, 1993). Studies of adolescents show increased risk of a range of symptoms of poor health in those whose parenting was characterised by hostility and rejection or conflict (Wickrama, Lorenz and Conger, 1997; Holler and Hurrelmann, 1990).

Parenting and minority ethnic families

It has been suggested that parents, irrespective of race, culture or class, have three primary goals. First to ensure their child's physical, social and emotional well-being. Second, to provide children with the economic competencies necessary for survival in adulthood, and third, to transmit the values of their culture (Levine, 1977 in Gross, 1996, p.178). Minority ethnic parents are faced with additional tasks as a result of their location within a culture that may be different to their own. These include preserving and transmitting aspects of their own value system in the face of a dominant culture which may be hostile to such values, and also helping their children to succeed in a society that may be hostile to such success in ways that are frequently covert (see Chapter 3 for further discussion).

It has been shown in the USA that some minority ethnic parents also face the problem that their children run a disproportionately high risk of a range of poor outcomes including early behaviour problems, school failure, and juvenile delinquency (e.g. Children's Defense Fund, 1985; Gibbs, 1984 in Myers, 1989). There is also an increased risk of the early initiation of substance abuse and of adolescent psychopathology (Kellam and others, 1983 in Myers and others, 1989). In the UK, black pupils are more likely to be permanently excluded from schools than children from any other ethnic group (e.g. 38 in every 10,000 black Caribbean children compared with 13 in every 10,000 white children or 3 in 10,000 Indian children), and are also less likely to do well in school (e.g. only half of black pupils achieved A*–C grade GCSEs compared with two-thirds of all other ethnic groups) (Office for National Statistics (ONS), 2002).

In addition to these extra parenting tasks, there is evidence to suggest that while the proportion of minority ethnic families in the UK is growing (minority ethnic families now represent 7.6 per cent of the total population – an increase of 44 per cent between 1991 and 2001) (ONS, 2002) they are still disproportionately represented in terms of social deprivation. Unemployment rates are between two and three times higher for most minority ethnic men than for white men (e.g. unemployment ranged between 25 and 31 per cent for young Black African men, Pakistanis, Black Caribbeans, and men of mixed origins compared with 12 per cent for whites) (ibid.). Pakistani and Bangladeshi households are more heavily reliant on social security benefits, which makes up nearly a fifth of their income (ibid.). People from minority ethnic groups are therefore more likely than white people to live in low income households. For example, almost 60 per cent of Pakistani and Bangladeshi families and 49 per cent of Black Non-Caribbean families live in low income households after housing costs have been deducted compared with 21 per cent of white families (ibid.). Members of minority ethnic groups are also more likely to be victims of racially motivated incidents, there being almost 280,000 such incidents in 1999. The highest risk was for Pakistani and Bangladeshi people (4.2 per cent), followed by Indian (3.6 per cent) and black people (2.2 per cent) compared with 0.3 per cent for white people (ONS, 2002).

Policy context

Increased recognition of the impact of parenting, particularly as regards criminality, violence and antisocial behaviour, has supported an increased emphasis on parenting and the family in the government's policy agenda (Henricson, 2003). Recent developments include the establishment of the Home Office's Family Policy Unit, and the independent National Family and Parenting Institute, as well as large national initiatives such as Sure Start, the Youth Justice Board's national parenting programme, and On Track. The evaluation of the relationship of parenting skills to children's behaviour and the development of strategies to improve the parenting of young children was highlighted as a research priority by the Department of Health (DH), as part of their strategy to improve the health of mothers and children (DH, 1995). A further NHS research priority identified by the Department was studies of the efficacy and cost-effectiveness of psychological treatments for emotional and behavioural problems in young people (ibid.).

Concentration among policy makers on the impact of parenting on crime and disorder has resulted in an emphasis on the value of optimal parenting for 'society' as opposed to its value for parents and children. The high costs to society of looking after and educating children with emotional and behavioural disorders (Scott and others, 2001a) are also advanced as an argument for societal support for parenting initiatives. Parenting initiatives have been viewed by some as a way of shifting the blame onto parents themselves for problems arising from the unpropitious economic and social circumstances in which many parents find themselves bringing up their children (Taylor, Spencer and Baldwin, 2000). This emphasis on the benefits of parenting interventions for society has deflected attention away from the increasing volume of research which shows that many parents want help and support with parenting, and that they value parenting education and support because it improves their emotional well-being and relationships with their children (Patterson and others, 2002; Barlow and Stewart-Brown, 2001). In this context it is perhaps not surprising that potentially helpful government policies to support the parenting of black and minority ethnic families, such as for example Modernising Social Services (DH, 1998) and Excellence Not Excuses (DH, 2000), have been interpreted in some circles as victim blaming or even racist.

It is within this somewhat conflicting policy context that the need for evidence concerning the effects of parenting programmes on parents from minority ethnic groups has emerged. Perhaps most importantly, while firmly acknowledging the centrality of family relationships for the development of communities and social capital, the main concerns of this review are with the benefits of parenting programmes for parents and children themselves, and not the intended or unintended benefits that may accrue from such interventions for society more generally.

Aims of the review

The aim of this review was to identify, critically appraise, and synthesise the evidence from quantitative and qualitative research studies of parenting programmes that had been delivered to minority ethnic parents.

The review aimed to address three questions.

■ What minority ethnic parents' experiences are of taking part in a parenting programme (Chapter 4).
■ Whether parenting programmes are as effective with parents from minority ethnic groups as they are with dominant western groups (Chapter 5).
■ Whether culturally specific parenting programmes are more effective than traditional parenting programmes (Chapter 5).

A search was conducted for parenting programmes that are delivered on a group basis, that use a standardised format and can therefore be repeated by others, and that are delivered specifically with the intention of supporting parents by improving parenting attitudes and practices, the well-being or relationship of parents and children, or family life more generally. The focus was on parenting programmes that have been specifically provided for parents from minority ethnic groups. Minority ethnic groups in this context refers to parents from African, Asian, or Hispanic cultures for example, who are living in predominantly British, American or

European societies. The review does not include programmes in which there is a cultural mix of parents from majority and minority ethnic groups unless the participants from the majority ethnic group (i.e. white parents) represent less than 20 per cent of the total. The reasons for this are that it is not possible to reach any conclusions about the specific effects of parenting programmes for minority ethnic parents where a large proportion of the sample are white. Due to the wide range of factors on which parenting can have an impact, this review has included studies examining any outcome, in order to identify the ways in which parenting programmes might help parents and children, as well as the ways in which they might be helpful to society in general.

2. Parenting programmes

Background

The increasing body of literature on helpful and unhelpful parenting styles and practices has supported the development of a range of interventions for parents. Approaches to provision are broad, including home visiting programmes, children's centres, family therapy, parenting programmes, parent support groups, books and television programmes. In this report we focus on just one of these approaches – parenting education and support programmes (also called parent training programmes). Over the last 20 years a range of these programmes have been developed and researched and there has been a rapid increase in their use both by statutory and non-statutory organisations (Pugh, De'Ath and Smith, 1994; Patterson and others, 2002). They are usually provided to parents in groups, involving meetings of around two hours a week and lasting 10 to 12 weeks. These programmes are gaining acceptance with the general population of parents. A recent survey in the South East of England showed that as many as one in five parents had attended a parenting programme, and that over half wanted the opportunity to attend such a programme in the future (Patterson and others, 2002).

There is a growing body of literature about the effectiveness of parenting programmes. Much of this research has been summarised in reviews, which have confirmed that parenting programmes can improve many aspects of family life including parents' well-being and parent–child relationships (e.g. Barlow, Coren and Stewart-Brown, 2002; Barlow and Stewart-Brown, 2000; Serketich and Dumas, 1996; Todres and Bunston, 1993; Cedar and Levant, 1990). In addition, qualitative research exploring parents' views about parenting programmes also shows favourable results (Barlow and Stewart-Brown, 2001; Stone, McKenry and Clark, 1999; Todis and others, 1993; Grimshaw and McGuire, 1998; Webster-Stratton and Spitzer, 1996). Some of these studies show that parents like group-based programmes because of the support that they receive from other parents, in addition to the mirroring of concerns on the part of other parents (e.g. Barlow and Stewart-Brown, 2001). As a result of the fact that many of the existing evaluations have been carried out with parents who are predominantly white, however, it has been concluded that these positive findings are not generalisable to minority ethnic parents (see for example, Barlow, Coren and Stewart-Brown, 2002).

It has been suggested that no parenting programme can be truly value-free (Smith, 1996, p.54), and that both the programme developers and the programme facilitators have their own value-laden 'baggage', which informs the content of the programme and the way in which it is delivered (ibid.). While many programmes are underpinned by broadly democratic values such as equality, respect, empathy, etc., some are underpinned by more traditional and highly specific values such as those of the Judaeo-Christian religion (e.g. Family Caring Trust and Positive Parenting Packs). The values underpinning most programmes, however, are not made explicit, and both programme developers and facilitators often make assumptions about families and parenting which may not be representative or valid. There has only been limited recognition to date of the potential problems with parenting programmes as regards gender-role, race, and religious stereotyping (see for example, Smith, 1996).

There is increasing recognition that parenting programmes are more likely to recruit white parents and that minority ethnic parents who volunteer to take part in such programmes are more likely to drop out prematurely (Farrington, 1991; Holden, Lavigne and Cameron, 1990; Strain, Young and Horowitz, 1981). The issue of low uptake and high drop out from traditional parenting programmes on the part of minority ethnic parents may reflect the mismatch between their experiences of being a parent, and programmes which have been designed with the sociocultural needs of White-European parents in mind. It has been suggested that traditional parenting programmes may be of questionable utility for minority ethnic parents (Alvy, 1987 in Myers and others, 1992). Research by the Race Equality Unit (REU) (Butt and Box, 1998) has shown that many minority ethnic families in the UK feel that parenting programmes are 'not for them' and that this is due in part to the way in which parenting techniques and strategies are presented (ibid.). This may mean that the needs of large sections of the population are being ignored or poorly met by existing parenting programmes (Myers and others, 1992).

Types of parenting programme

Two main types of parenting programme have been defined – behavioural and 'relationship' programmes (Smith, 1996). Behavioural parenting programmes are based on social learning theory (i.e. behaviourism) and focus on helping parents to improve their children's behaviour using methods such as praise to encourage 'good' behaviour and ignoring to discourage 'bad' behaviour. Relationship parenting programmes include all of the non-behavioural programmes, and as such represent a rather diverse group. They include for example, Adlerian programmes, communication based programmes and psychodynamic programmes.

Some parenting programmes are directed at particular groups of parents. For example, incarcerated or single parents, or parents of children with learning disabilities or chronic illness. Parenting programmes that are directed at parents from minority ethnic groups represent part of this diversity.

Parenting programmes for minority ethnic parents

While many family interventions ignore racial and ethnic diversity (Slaughter, 1983), some 'culturally sensitive' parenting programmes have been developed (Rowland and Wampler, 1983). For example, the Effective Black Parenting Programme (EBPP), which is widely used in the USA, comprises units that specifically address the experiences of black parents. One such unit entitled 'Pride in Blackness' involves discussion with parents on topics such as culture and history and ways for parents to communicate positively about being black and dealing with racism. A further unit encourages the use of a number of methods described as 'Modern Black Self-Discipline' with their links with the civil rights and Black Power movements, in contrast to the use of methods that are described as 'Traditional Black Discipline' and corporal punishment which, it is suggested, have their roots in slavery.

Three main types of parenting programmes for minority ethnic parents have been identified (Cheng Gorman, 1996 in Cheng Gorman and Balter, 1997) – 'translated', 'adapted' and 'culturally specific'. The following panel depicts the approach of the three types of programme.

> **Types of parenting programmes for minority ethnic parents**
>
> ■ **Translated programmes** – traditional parent education programmes which have been translated into a target population's native language, but which are essentially unchanged from the original programme.
>
> ■ **Adapted programmes** – traditional parent education programmes that have been modified to include some of the values and traditions of the target population.
>
> ■ **Culturally specific programmes** – parenting programmes that have been designed to incorporate the values of the target population.

Both adapted and culturally specific parenting programmes may be defined as 'culturally sensitive' in that they take the specific cultural needs of the participants into account. The term 'culturally sensitive' will be used throughout the remainder of this book as a generic term to refer to all parenting programmes that take account of the ethnicity of the participants (i.e. culturally adapted and culturally specific programmes). It should be noted that the term is also used below to define a parenting programme aimed at multi-ethnic groups as opposed to being culturally specific or adapted.

There are currently few 'culturally specific' parenting programmes available in the UK. The Moyenda Black Families Project (Hylton, 1997) is one notable example. In addition, the REU has adapted an American parenting programme for minority ethnic families, and is currently introducing it in various locations throughout the UK. The fact that there is little research on these programmes in the UK means that there may be much that we can learn from research conducted in other countries such as the US. What can be learnt will depend on the extent to which it is possible to transfer the findings across different cultural contexts, and this is discussed again in the Chapter 6.

Parenting programmes identified by the review

The studies identified in this review covered a wide range of programmes, some of which are well known and some of which are not. Some of the well-known programmes have been shortened, adapted or modified, and some have been translated. The final section of this chapter 'Parenting programmes included in the review' presents a description of the programmes evaluated in each of the studies with a summary of the content and delivery of the programme.

The studies identified covered a wide range of parenting programmes. Both behavioural and relationship programmes were represented. Most of the studies evaluated traditional or translated parenting programmes and relatively few evaluated culturally sensitive parenting programmes. Most of the latter were culturally specific programmes and the majority of these studies evaluated the effectiveness of the Effective Black Parenting Programme. A small number of studies evaluated the effectiveness of culturally adapted programmes. However, details about the ways in which the programme had been adapted were sparse.

Study ID	Parenting programme(s) studied and description of participants	Content and method of delivery of programme
Culturally specific programmes		
Akinyela (1996)	The Ujamaa Circle Process: Conscious Parenting Family Circles.	The programme aimed to draw on the participants' experiences and address how such experiences fit into the dominant American culture. Delivered using structured dialogue. 10 to 12 weekly, 1½ to 2 hour sessions.
Myers and others (1992) 2 cohorts	Effective Black Parenting Programme (EBPP) with Inner City African-American Families.	The programme contains a variety of behavioural child management skills within a black achievement perspective known as 'Pyramid of Success for Black Children'. Families taught two child-rearing strategies – a family rule guideline strategy and 'Thinking Parents' approach. Also includes other topics such as 'Pride in Blackness'. 15 sessions.
Pitts (2001)	Modified version of Effective Black Parenting Programme, with children exhibiting severe conduct problems.	Modified version of the EBPP – see Myers and others (1992). Seven 1½-hour sessions.
Norwood and others (1997)	Culturally responsive programme for urban parents.	The programme was developed collaboratively with African-American parents. Consisted of two key components: (a) standard behaviour management training and (b) ways of helping children to learn at home. Each session contained a lecture, followed by a discussion and demonstration exercise. Eight 2-hour weekly sessions.

Parenting programmes included in the review

Steele and others (2002)	Strengthening Families Strengthening Communities Programme – summary of the outcome of 143 different projects containing 449 different classes (SMFC). Note: This is a culturally sensitive (i.e. non-specific) parenting programme.	The programme aimed to improve children's social competence, help parents and children to manage conflict, and included sessions on dealing with the wider community. Normally 12 (but sometimes 8 or 10) 2- to 3-hour sessions.
Thomas (2000)	Effective Black Parenting Programme (EBPP).	The programme was based on EBPP – see Myers and others (1992). Includes modules on traditional black discipline versus modern black self-discipline, developing self-esteem and 'pride in blackness'. 15 sessions.
Ying (1999)	Programme designed to reduce intergenerational conflict in migrant families (SITCAF).	The programme aimed to help parents understand the cultural differences between their own and European American cultures, and stressed the ways in which children might feel divided between the two cultures. The programme included sessions from more traditional parenting programmes. The course was taught entirely in Mandarin. Eight 2-hour weekly sessions.

Culturally adapted parenting programmes

Alvy (1988)	Parent Effectiveness Training (PET), Systematic Training for Effective Parenting (STEP), and Confident Parenting with African-American parents.	The standard programmes were modified to meet the needs and requirements of the black community. The rationale for why black parents should participate was illustrated by using the 'Pyramid of Success', which links parents' life goals for their children to the abilities and characteristics children need in order to achieve them, and to the behaviours parents must model and teach to develop the desired child attributes. The standard skills taught in these programmes were related to the pyramid. Units added included 'pride in blackness' and 'traditional versus modern black discipline'. 15 sessions.
Carten (1986)	Independent Life Skills Preparation Project and Communication Interaction Programme for foster parents.	The programme was designed to help foster parents improve their fostering skills, and included modules on human development, behaviour management, and black family lifestyles. Eight weekly 2-hour sessions.

Davis (1994)	Modified Systematic Training for Effective Parenting programme (STEP) with Hispanic parents whose children were students enrolled in a bilingual education programme.	A STEP programme was modified to be consistent with Hispanic culture, and included the following sessions: Understanding children's behaviour; The good parent versus responsible parent; Encouragement versus praise; Communication; Expressing ideas and feelings; Natural and logical consequences; Decision making for parents; The family meeting. Four 2-hour weekly sessions.
Villegas (1977)	Standard Adlerian parent training programme.	Programme included the following sessions: Understanding behaviour and misbehaviour; Children's four motives for involving parents; Encouragement; Communication: listening; Communication: exploring alternatives; Developing responsibility; Decision making for parents; The family meeting; Developing confidence and your potential. Seven 2-hour sessions.

Culturally adapted parenting programmes

Chau and Landrath (1997) Chau (1996)	Filial therapy training for Chinese parents.	The programme aimed to enhance parent–child relationships by teaching parents to create an accepting environment through which children would feel safe to express and explore their feelings. The programme was taught through didactic instruction, demonstration, and role-play. Ten weekly 2-hour sessions.
Leal (1985)	Several different unnamed programmes.	Several different parenting programmes were evaluated. All included hand-outs and brochures and were based on small group discussions following major presentations. 10 or 12 sessions of 1 or 2 hours, conducted once or twice a week.
Reid, Webster-Stratton and Beauchaine (2001)	Incredible Years Parenting Programme for low-income sample of Caucasian, African-American, Hispanic, and Asian mothers whose children were enrolled in Head Start.	The programme taught child-directed play skills, positive discipline strategies, effective parenting skills, strategies for coping with stress, and ways to strengthen children's prosocial and social skills. If sufficient participants were available the programme was taught in Spanish or Vietnamese. Methods used included videotapes, group discussions, and role-play. Groups ranged in length from 8 to 12 weekly sessions.

| Yuen (1997) | Filial Therapy for Chinese Canadian parents. | The programme aimed to enhance parent–child relationships by helping parents learn how to create an accepting environment in which their children would feel safe enough to express and explore thoughts and feelings. The skills were taught using dyadic instruction, demonstration and role-play, and the parents also conducted a weekly 30-minute play session with their children at home. The sessions were taught in Cantonese. Ten 2-hour weekly sessions. |

Traditional parenting programmes

Berman and Rickel (1979)	Bespoke parenting programme that aimed to increase the self-esteem of family members.	The parents were taught how to listen, make requests, discipline, and resolve conflict with their children using games and role-play. Parents were encouraged to practise their skills each day for 10 minutes as part of homework assignments. Five weekly and one follow-up session of $2^{1/2}$ hours.
Booker (1986)	Short-term parent education programme for low-income black adolescent single teenage mothers.	The programme was designed for pregnant and parenting teenagers, and aimed to increase their understanding of parenthood, child development, and other child-rearing skills. The course was taught using instruction, role-play and discussion. Five weekly sessions of 2 hours.
Cox (2002)	Empowerment programme for African-American grandparents.	The programme was aimed at increasing grandparents' empowerment and improving their communication skills with grandchildren. Included the following sessions: Introduction to empowerment; Importance of self-esteem; Communicating with grandchildren; Dealing with loss and grief; Helping grandchildren deal with loss; Dealing with behaviour problems; Talking to grandchildren about sex, HIV/AIDS and drugs; Legal and entitlement issues; Developing advocacy skills; Negotiating systems; Making presentations and a review. Twelve classes of unknown length and frequency.
Copeland (1981)	Exploring Parenting Curriculum.	The programme used group discussions, case studies, observation, role-play, brainstorming, and skills practice to help parents to get to know themselves and their children better, and to use this knowledge in decision making. The programme was delivered over 20 sessions of unknown length and frequency.

Creswell-Betsch (1979)	Micro training and a reading material based programme.	The programme taught parents to listen to and understand their children and respond to them in a more empathetic manner. Sessions included the following: Introduction; Micro training; Basic attending skills; Reflection of behaviour and verbal content; Reflection of feelings; Empathic problem solving. Information was presented using lectures, live or videotaped demonstrations and exercises that included simulated parent–child interactions using role-play. Four 2-hour weekly sessions.
Day (1995)	A programme designed to give parents the skills to protect their children from substance abuse.	The programme aimed to give parents the skills to help protect their adolescent children from substance abuse through improving skills in communication and providing positive influences. In addition it helped parents identify resources and sources of support in their own community. Sessions included: Coming together; The importance of communication; Why families count; How values influence behaviour; Outside influences; Guiding teen behaviour (discipline); Getting help; Where do we go from here. The programme was based on approximately 15 units, which were designed to be presented using different formats.
Glover and Landreth (2000)	Filial Therapy model for Native American parents residing on the Flathead reservation in Montana.	The programme aimed to improve self-esteem and the feelings underlying inappropriate behaviour. The parents were taught to conduct special play sessions modelled on child-centred play therapy. The programme was delivered using dyadic instruction, videotapes, and role-play. Ten 2-hour weekly sessions.
Gordon-Rosen (1982) Gordon-Rosen and Rosen (1984)	Standard Adlerian Parent Study Group using STEP materials for parents of black junior high school children.	Parents taught the four main reasons for children misbehaving, and encouraged to read chapters from 'Children: the Challenge' at home. Class time was devoted to discussion of this material along with appropriate material from the STEP kits. The sessions included discussion and role-play. Nine 2-hour weekly sessions.

Levant and Slattery (1982) Levant and Slobodian (1981)	Systematic skills training programme for inner-city, lower socio-economic minority group foster mothers.	The programme included sessions on: Attending; Listening and responding; Speaking for oneself; Genuineness; Acceptance; Structuring; Rules, limits and consequences; Conflict resolution; Integration; and Skilled foster parenting. The methods used included videotaped and live demonstrations, role-play, and homework assignments. Ten 3-hour weekly sessions.
Mendez-Baldwin (2001)	Parent education workshop for Low-Income Head Start Parents.	The programme included sessions on communication, discipline and behaviour management. New skills were presented and rehearsed using role-play. In addition there were discussions of the parents' specific problems. Three or more $\frac{1}{2}$-hour weekly sessions.
Nicholson and others (2002)	STAR – a psychoeducational parenting programme for parents of low socio-economic status who use excessive verbal and corporal punishment.	The programme was based on a cognitive-behavioural approach. The first part of the programme taught how young children influence parents' thoughts and feelings and parents are taught a more thoughtful way to respond. The second part focused on child development and encouraged realistic parent expectations. The third and fourth parts of the programme focused on positive parenting and discipline strategies. Ten weekly $\frac{1}{2}$-hour sessions.
Percy and McIntyre (2001)	Programme to improve parent self-confidence in teenage mothers.	The programme was designed to improve teenage parents' knowledge of the course of pregnancy and child development, and how the mother's relationship would change with family and friends. The programme was taught using a semi-structured discussion format. Fifteen 1-hour weekly sessions.
Parker Scott (1999)	Parent education programmes for parents of male juveniles.	The programmes included sessions about the structure of the family, responsibility, addiction, and communication. On completion the parents had the option of participating in a monthly support group with other parents. 20 sessions.
Pembroke (1980)	Parent education programme to improve children's self-concept and moral reasoning.	The programme aimed to promote communication and ways of resolving conflict within families, relating this to children's social and moral reasoning. Delivered using presentations and role-play. Eight 2-hour weekly sessions.

Shure and Spivack (1978)	Interpersonal Cognitive Problem Solving Skills programme.	The programme was designed to teach parents to teach their children problem solving skills. Consisted of ten 3-hour weekly sessions.
Slaughter (1983)	Mothers' Discussion Group.	The Mothers' Discussion Group was aimed at improving children's social and emotional development by allowing mothers to discuss their experiences of rearing children. The groups ran during term time for two years.
Wolfe (1997) (2 studies)	Listening to Children Programme.	The programme was based on the theory and practice of Re-evaluation Counselling, and aimed to help parents to re-evaluate their experiences and current practices and provide parents with new methods and guidelines for raising children. Methods included lectures, small group discussions, and homework sessions. Eight 2½-hour weekly sessions.
Tulloch (1996)	SOS behavioural parent training programme for parents of ethnic minority preschoolers from low SES families.	A video taped based behavioural management programme. Five 2-hour sessions.

Comparison of programmes

Moore (1992)	Preparing for the Drug Free Years (PDFY) and Parents Reclaiming African Information for Spiritual Enlightenment (PRAISE).	Preparing for Drug Free Years (PDFY) aimed to provide positive, stronger overall family bonds to prevent children from using drugs, using lectures, discussions, worksheets and homework assignments. Consisted of five sessions.
		Parents Reclaiming African Information for Spiritual Enlightenment (PRAISE) included sessions on improving parent–child communication, developing pride in blackness, coping with racism. The programme was delivered using lectures, discussions, presentations and homework assignments. 12 sessions.
Perez-Nieves (2001)	Behavioural programme and a Rational Emotive Therapy programme (REBT).	The rational emotive behaviour therapy focused on teaching parents how to control their emotions and to handle their children's behaviour. Delivered using role-play to demonstrate effective parenting skills. Modifications for use with Hispanic populations were made.

		The behavioural programme was based on basic behaviour management principles, in addition to the use of English and Spanish worksheets. Both programmes consisted of four weekly sessions.
Schutt-Aine (1994)	Parent to Parent Programme (PTP) and Effective Black Parenting Programme (EBPP).	Parent to Parent Programme (PTP) focused on parenting issues such as the influence of drugs on children, and emphasised changing parent fatalistic beliefs into positive ones. Information was presented using videotapes followed by discussion. Eight 2-hour sessions conducted over 12 weeks.
		Modified Effective Black Parenting Programme EBPP – see Myers and others, 1992. Seven 1½-hour sessions.

3. Methodological issues

Introduction

The search strategy was wide ranging (see Appendix 1) and the findings of this review are based on data obtained from both qualitative (Chapter 4) and quantitative (Chapter 5) studies. The following sections describe some of the methodological issues involved.

The review aimed to identify all published and unpublished studies of parenting programmes delivered to minority ethnic parents both in groups and individually.

Qualitative methodology

Qualitative studies are an important means of obtaining valid 'insider' accounts of particular phenomena. Thus, while qualitative studies tend to have poor external validity (i.e. generalisability) because they are undertaken with small unrepresentative samples, they nevertheless have good internal validity (i.e. truth value) because they permit the collection of a richer and more valid type of data. While systematic reviews of quantitative studies are now common, the summary of data from qualitative studies is still in its infancy (Sandelowski, Docherty and Emden, 1997). The development of rationale and standards for the systematic review of qualitative literature is also still being developed (Popay, Rogers and Williams, 1998). Qualitative synthesis (sometimes call meta-ethnography – e.g. Noblitt, Hare and Noblit, 1988), does not aim to aggregate findings from studies as is the case with quantitative reviews (meta-analyses), rather to be interpretive (i.e. to maintain the focus on the perspectives and experiences of the people being studied). A synthesis of qualitative studies thus aims to go beyond single accounts to reveal the analogies between the accounts. It reduces the accounts, while preserving the sense of the account through the selection of key metaphors and organisers. (ibid., p.13)

For the purpose of this review therefore, the findings from the 12 qualitative studies were synthesised through the 'reciprocal translation of metaphors' method in which the themes from the different studies were translated and compared across studies, and then synthesised by determining which themes were able to encompass those of other accounts (ibid.). This approach is similar to the 'constant comparative method' that is used to analyse primary qualitative data. The key themes emerging from the studies have been presented and representative quotations on each of the themes from one or more of the studies have been presented (see Chapter 4).

Quantitative methodology

Quantitative studies are better placed than qualitative studies to provide evidence concerning whether a particular intervention (in this case parenting programmes) is effective. The value of combining results from quantitative studies in reviews is that we are able to get a better overall picture of whether an intervention is effective rather than relying on the results of much smaller studies which may be too limited to enable generalisation (ibid.). However, some quantitative methodologies (i.e. the more rigorous controlled studies) are better placed than others (i.e. one group designs) to provide evidence concerning the effectiveness of an intervention and for this reason reviews very often exclude evidence from less rigorous designs. The current review included all studies irrespective of the research methodology used. The reasons for this were that we wished to obtain a picture of the diversity of programmes being used with minority ethnic parents, and were concerned that limiting the studies to be included might distort the picture. We also suspected that there might not be many rigorous (i.e. controlled) studies available.

The review is therefore based on a range of methodologies. The least rigorous group of studies to be included are one-group designs in which researchers measured some attribute of parenting prior to the implementation of a parenting programme and then repeated the measurement at the end of the programme to identify changes between the two points in time. One of the difficulties in interpreting the results of these studies is that parents often make changes to their parenting without the help of parenting programmes and it is therefore impossible to be sure that any changes that are identified happened as a result of the programme. The advantages are that these studies are relatively inexpensive and easy to carry out, and are therefore within the resources of many programme developers and postgraduate students. As a result, they tend to be more numerous.

In order to ensure that it is possible to attribute changes to a particular programme, however, it is necessary to include a group of parents who do not receive the programme and to compare the changes in the two groups, i.e. those who receive the programme with those who do not. If greater change is observed in the programme group than the control group it is possible to have more confidence that the findings are attributable to the intervention. Studies such as these can enhance the quality of their results by taking account of differences between control and treatment groups at the start of the trial, i.e. adjusting for these differences statistically.

Interpretation of the results of controlled trials may nevertheless be problematic because parents who elect to take part in parenting programmes are more likely to change than those that do not. Randomised controlled trials (RCTs) in which parents are randomly allocated to attend a programme or act as a control can surmount this problem. They can also surmount the problem of investigator bias in which researchers wittingly or unwittingly allocate parents who are likely to change to programme groups, and those who are not likely to change, to control groups. For these reasons RCTs are regarded as the optimum methodology for quantitative study designs. However, this design is more readily applicable to drug trials than it is to interventions which depend on people making changes to their lives. Participants in the latter can find it hard to understand why they should be asked to take part in what they see as a lottery, and why it is that a programme that is thought to be helpful is only available to some. Many potential participants therefore elect not to take part in such trials, and this can result in the recruitment of atypical groups of parents. High levels of refusal from RCTs can reduce the utility of such studies to such an extent that the results may be meaningless. RCTs can also be beset by other problems. For example, the process of taking part in a study with the resulting reflection on parenting that such participation necessarily involves can sometimes result in change in the control group. RCTs can also be very expensive and are beyond the resources of many programme developers.

In addition to study design, the size of a study can be important. On the whole, large studies are more rigorous than small studies because the results are less subject to chance findings. However, large studies can be more difficult to carry out and are inevitably more expensive. The problem of attrition from studies is also important and can be as high as 50 per cent in evaluations of parenting programmes. One of the consequences of high attrition is a reduction in the generalisability of the findings. The value of a study is also dependent on the measurements that are made. Quantitative studies have to rely on standardised measures, some of which are not always suitable (i.e. they have often been designed to measure change in clinical populations), and some of which have been developed in ways that do not ensure their reliability and validity. The more measures a researcher uses, the more likely they are to find a positive result by chance, but the less likely they are to miss important findings.

It is therefore important that the limitations of different studies are borne in mind when interpreting the results, and for this reason the methodological limitations of studies are described below.

Methodological limitations of included studies

Qualitative studies

The quality of many of the qualitative studies was variable. For example, some studies did not provide details concerning the way in which the data were collected, the number of parents who provided data, or information concerning the demographic characteristics of the parents. In addition, many studies did not address the extent to which the data were valid (i.e. whether the respondents were appropriate and representative), whether the data were dependable (i.e. whether coding of data, etc., was undertaken reliably), or the transferability of the data (i.e. to what extent the data were context bound). In a number of studies, the data consisted entirely of author's comments concerning the participants' experiences. The consequence of this is that the internal (and external) validity of the data that are presented in Chapter 4 may have been compromised.

Quantitative studies

The methodological quality of some of the quantitative studies was also variable. While ten studies were RCTs, at least one involved quasi-random allocation to groups, in a number of cases the method of allocation was not specified, and some of the studies did not have sufficiently large numbers in order to detect significant changes (i.e. were underpowered). In a number of the controlled studies no matching was undertaken, and no adjustment for confounders. Furthermore, in at least one case, post-intervention scores for the intervention and control group were compared, despite the absence of matching or adjustment. In the case of one-group designs, the major methodological problem is that it is not possible to assess, in the absence of a control group, to what extent the change that was observed would have occurred anyway. While the four comparative studies provide a useful assessment of the relative effectiveness of different types of parenting programmes (see below for further discussion), none of these studies utilised a control group and it is not therefore possible to know if the observed change would have occurred anyway.

There were, in addition, a number of other methodological problems. Some studies did not report all of the outcomes, and most studies did not include any independent assessments of outcome. A number of studies measured outcomes that are unlikely to have been affected by the intervention in the short-term, e.g. children's educational achievement. Many of the included studies were undertaken as part of PhD studentships, and the quality of these is variable. Perhaps most significantly, it seems likely that many of the PhD theses were conducted with a view to exploring interesting hypotheses, as opposed to conducting comprehensive evaluations of the effectiveness of a parenting programme, and this is sometimes reflected in, for example, the number and type of outcome measures used.

The implication of the above methodological issues is that significant caution should be attached to the findings of some of the included studies.

Summary

The studies included in this review describe the many ways in which parenting programmes can help parents. The data from the small number of qualitative studies confirm the findings of the more numerous quantitative studies and provide a broader insight into the ways in which parents find such programmes helpful. Although the quality of some of the studies was poor and none of them include the views of parents who dropped out of the programmes, such data provide both programme providers and policy makers with the necessary insights to begin to address the ways in which parenting programmes could be adapted to meet the needs of all parents in a multicultural society. The exclusion of less rigorous studies might have prevented us from gaining an understanding of the full diversity of programmes available. We have therefore endeavoured to give more credit to the results of better quality studies.

4. The experiences of minorit ethnic parents who take part in a parenting programme

Introduction

One of the central tasks of parenting, in addition to providing the necessary conditions for physical, social and emotional development, is the socialisation of children. One of the main aims of socialisation is the transmission of the parents' values and beliefs to their children (Gross, 1996). This can be difficult where the parents' values, beliefs, and cultural background are different from those of the mainstream society within which they live. Minority ethnic children are as such required to adapt to two cultures (i.e. that of their parents and that of the society within which they are located) often when members of their family may still be feeling conflicted or ambivalent about the dominant culture (ibid.). As a result of their experience of living with two cultures, minority ethnic children develop a bi-cultural identity. This has been described as a psychosocial process experienced by members of a subordinate culture living within a dominant culture that devalues the content and meaning of the subordinate culture (Akinyela, 1996, pp.44–5). Bi-cultural identify is therefore both a survival response to marginalisation and an affirmation of cultural identity, and perhaps most importantly it provides minority ethnic children with 'a range of ways of relating to the dominant culture and culturally moderated ways of thinking and problem solving' (ibid., pp.44–5).

In addition to developing a bi-cultural identity, minority ethnic children are likely to encounter socio-economic barriers and restricted opportunities as a result of both overt and covert (institutional) racism. It has been suggested that this 'second-class status' resembles a caste-class system that is significantly different from social class disadvantage in that it cannot be improved by education or income, and continues throughout the child's life (Thomas, 2000). These problems can be compounded by the absence of positive role models and the exposure of some minority ethnic children to negative images and ideas that are internalised, and which may then inhibit their capacity to take on adult roles (ibid., p.49).

Minority ethnic parents may thereby be faced with the task of both preserving and transmitting their cultural values and beliefs in the face of an often hostile dominant culture, and of preparing their children to succeed in a society which may militate against such success in ways which are often covert. They are as such required to undertake a number of parenting tasks that are not required of parents who are part of the dominant culture.

The majority of (traditional) parenting programmes are based on the values of white, middle class culture and issues relating to cultural and socio-economic context are rarely addressed. Thus, for example, many programmes make no references to different family structures (i.e. extended rather than nuclear families), no mention of the ethnic or cultural heritage of families, both of which will have played a significant part in influencing parenting techniques and family arrangements (Thomas, 2000, p.45), and provide 'no sense of relationship to any cultural or ethnic community within the larger society' (ibid.). The usefulness of such programmes for minority ethnic parents has therefore been questioned (Alvy, 1988).

This chapter aims to synthesise the results of qualitative studies about minority ethnic parents' experiences of taking part in a parenting programme. It sets the scene for understanding the results of the quantitative studies that follow and provides insights into the ways that parenting programmes can be helpful. The first part of the chapter draws together the common themes from the studies and describes the experiences of parents. It also explores evidence about whether there is a difference in minority ethnic parents' experience of traditional and culturally specific programmes. The focus of the second part of the chapter is on how minority ethnic parents feel about parenting programmes that may advocate practices underpinned by values that are in conflict with those of their own culture, and what culturally specific parenting programmes may offer parents over and above traditional parenting programmes.

Twelve qualitative studies were identified, although only 11 provided data, concerning the experiences of parents attending traditional or culturally specific programmes. One study evaluated a traditional parenting programme that had been translated into Chinese but there were no studies of culturally adapted programmes. Most of the quotations in the following sections are from African-American parents. This is due to the fact that most of the available data were provided by a small number of studies, the majority of which addressed the experiences of African-American parents. Chinese-American and Native American parents are also represented to a lesser extent.

Experiences of taking part in a parenting programme

Many of the studies provided data about parents' reasons for taking part in a parenting programme, and their expectations at the start of the programme. The next section presents the findings of this aspect of the data, followed by a section that examines the benefits parents reported from taking part in a parenting programme. There then follows a section that examines the aspects of parenting programmes that parents experienced as helpful. The final section summarises the problems that parents experienced and the aspects of parenting programmes that they did not like.

All of the quotations indicate the parent's ethnicity and the type of parenting programme in which they have participated. The small number of studies, however, precluded the possibility of analysing the results by ethnic group, and readers who have a particular interest in the experiences of a particular ethnic group may find it beneficial to read the original studies (see references).

Motivation and expectations

Motivations for taking part

There were a number of reasons why minority ethnic parents took part in a parenting programme. These included the desire to learn more about parenting and the need to find better ways of dealing with children's behaviour:

> 'I wasn't educated about a lot of things as being a parent. I just
> went with the flow. I was going to start the course just because I
> thought that I liked to learn a little bit more to be able to parent
> my children properly.'
> *(Thomas 2000, p.130 [Culturally Specific, African-American])*

Grandparents were also keen to take part in parenting programmes. Some were looking for ways of dealing with the attitudes and behaviour of modern-day children, and were finding their earlier parenting experiences inadequate to the task. The participation of grandparents in parenting programmes is not common among white families, and the participation of minority ethnic grandparents may reflect the different family structures within minority ethnic groups in which grandparents, aunts, uncles and other relatives play a significant role in the rearing of children:

> 'I had raised a family at another point [in] time and am in the
> process of raising my grandchildren and the way I parented my
> own – was not it just wasn't working ... today the children are
> different.'
> *(Thomas, 2000, p.130 [Culturally Specific, African-American])*

In some cases, parents were attracted to culturally specific parenting programmes
because of the focus on black culture:

> 'I liked the fact that it focused especially on the African-
> American family and that's why I attend the class.'
> *(Thomas, 2000, p.130 [Culturally Specific, African-American])*

While the majority of minority ethnic parents volunteered to take part in a
parenting programme, there was also evidence to indicate that some parents were
legally required to take part as a result of a court mandate:

> 'I was told I would have to take a class in parenting, which I had
> asked for even before I was told I had to for my four
> granddaughters. And then I had to take a parenting class for my
> teenager.'
> *(Thomas, 2000, p.141 [Culturally Specific, African-American])*

> 'We, well, I can only speak for myself, my husband had spanked
> his daughter and the family service agency took the children out
> of his custody and that's why most of the reason why we're here.'
> *(Thomas, 2000, p.141 [Culturally Specific, African-American])*

The payment of stipends to deprived parents who agree to take part in parenting
programmes is a common feature of US parenting programmes, and in one study,
parents indicated that this was their main motivation for attending the programme:

> 'Once I attended the first class, I was happy to return. But I
> didn't expect that, and I wouldn't have signed up without the
> money.'
> *(Wolfe, 1997, p.91 [Traditional, African-American])*

Expectations about the programme

There was considerable variation in the expectations of minority ethnic parents
about parenting programmes, in particular with regard to who would be attending
and how they would relate to each other. There were also differences with regard to
expectations about the formality and structuring of the programmes:

'I thought it would be real structured. I thought someone would
dictate to us and give parenting statistics. I wasn't looking for it
come from a community approach.'
(Akinyela, 1996, p.233 [Culturally Specific, African-American])

Other parents, however, expected the programme to be much more supportive:

'I expected a lot of parents to participate. I was looking for
support. I had a lot of things on my mind.'
(Akinyela, 1996, p.235 [Culturally Specific, African-American])

Some of these expectations about parenting programmes were based on previous
experiences of taking part in a parenting programme. Akinyela (1996), who
specifically asked parents about their earlier experiences, showed that while some
parents had good earlier experiences, in some cases parents had bad experiences to
report:

'We have been to three different places observing parent groups.
In one group [the] speaker did all the talking. Parents weren't
allowed to talk or to ask questions. In another they had parent
work books and that was boring.'
(Akinyela, 1996, p.233 [Culturally Specific, African-American])

Given the fact that not all parents had volunteered to take part in some of the
parenting programmes, it might be expected that some parents would have mixed
feelings about being there:

'When I first came, I had a little attitude. Like, I don't wanna be
there and I don't wanna hear all that...'
(Wolfe, 1997, p.95 [Traditional, African-American])

Benefits of taking part in a parenting programme

Benefits to parents

Participation in a parenting programme appeared to have produced a number of
benefits for parents including enjoyment, introduction to new ideas, reduced stress,
greater self-control, and an increased sense of empowerment.

I'd keep the parent class I really do. I really do.'
(Wolfe, 1997, p.102 [Traditional, African-American])

New ideas

In some cases, there was evidence that participation in a parenting programme had been successful in introducing parents to new ideas:

> 'I mean this program opened my eyes to a lot of things that I
> would never – a lot of things I just didn't know.'
> *(Thomas, 2000, p.132 [Culturally Specific, African-American])*

The focus of most parenting programmes is on the parents themselves. Some parents were clear that having participated in a parenting programme, they themselves needed to change if their children and the wider community were going to change:

> 'Change must begin with the individuals before we can better
> our families and our communities … we need to get oneself in
> balance before we can be role models for our children. Walking
> in balance helps us to … make the right decisions that affect the
> majority in a family circle. I believe that by walking in balance
> with myself I would be better suited to take care of myself, my
> family, and my community.'
> *(Brave Heart, 1999, pp.199 [Culturally Specific, Native American])*

Less stress

One of the major benefits of taking part in a parenting programme for minority ethnic parents was feeling less stressed, more relaxed, and less prone to what one little boy described as his mum's 'temper tantrums':

> 'I have become more relaxed.'
> *(Gordon-Rosen, 1982, pp.113–14 [Traditional, African-American])*

> 'I took my son to McDonalds and mentioned that he had fewer
> temper tantrums lately. It was so funny that he said the same
> thing to me, that I had less temper tantrums. Choice giving really
> helps to decrease the power struggles between us. And I become
> more patient when I am not in a power struggle.'
> *(Chau, 1996, p.84 [Translated, Chinese])*

A number of parents felt that they had learned to be more forgiving towards themselves, and to recognise that they needed to be 'good enough' rather than 'perfect' parents:

> 'I'm more thoughtful about how I respond to my children and
> the things they do. I learned that you're taught these things so
> you gotta unteach yourself. I've learned to cut myself some slack.
> I don't need to do this perfect.'
> *(Thomas, 2000, p.132 [Culturally Specific, African-American])*

Cox (2002) found that the grandparents in his study liked the use of a cardboard 'feelings thermometer' as a way of indicating their own and their grandchildren's emotional state, and helping to relieve the tension.

Increased self-control

Minority ethnic parents expressed a number of ways in which they felt that their attitudes and behaviour had changed as a result of taking part in a parenting programme. One of the changes in behaviour that a number of parents referred to was an increase in self-control. This manifested itself in a number of ways including not 'yelling' at the children and having a more thoughtful approach to being a parent:

> 'The biggest change that I've finally made is that I've stopped
> yelling. My nickname was "yelling", because I'd soon be hollering
> at my kids all the time, and I'm able to pause, think through
> what they've done, determine a little bit better it's relative
> importance, whether it even makes sense for me to get excited
> about it anymore. And, being able to talk to them in regard why
> they're doing some things in relationship to our family rules, or
> how we already discussed how we want to conduct ourselves and
> get along with one another, and why they're not communicating
> or operating in that fashion at the time.'
> *(Thomas, 2000, p.132 [Culturally Specific, African-American])*

Feeling empowered

Parents also expressed feeling more empowered and confident. One facilitator of a culturally specific programme said 'I could see empowerment happening within the group' (Brave Heart 1999, p.121 [Culturally Specific, Native-American]). Two parents who had taken part in a traditional parenting programme provided examples of how they had used the knowledge and confidence that they had gained from the parenting programme in other arenas:

'...I find myself using what I learned in the class. I had to go to a meeting because there's a position open at [Head Start] and parents interview [the candidates]. Well! I threw in my little parenting skills that I learned. One of the questions that I asked was, "I took a parenting class and the first thing our group leader let us know was that there is no right or wrong and that's how she made us feel comfortable. We were able to open up to her right away. We had no problem." See, we were interviewing for a social worker. And I needed to know for myself whether I can feel comfortable with the new person that's coming in, so the question was, "Do you feel there's a right or wrong?" You know, so I was able to apply what I've learned in that area. And I felt really good about that. I really did and the applicant was very interested to hear that we had a parenting class and she asked a lot of questions about it.'

(Wolfe, 1997, p.100 [Traditional, African-American])

There was also some evidence to suggest that increased feelings of confidence and empowerment had lead to increased participation in the wider community. Berman and Rickel (1979) observed that parents had a more positive association with the school, and one parent in the Akinyela (1996) study stated:

'I've been going through addiction in last few years. But now I have confidence to become active now in PTA. Being in this little group kinda gave me incentive. I started getting in and things started happening.'

(Akinyela, 1996, p.235 [Culturally Specific, African-American])

Benefits for children

Participation in a parenting programme had also led to a number of benefits for children, including an improvement in parent–child communication as a result of an increase in the parent's ability to listen and talk to their children, an increase in the amount of time spent together, an increase in children's freedom and autonomy, increased empathy, and more positive methods of discipline.

Improved parent–child communications

Participation in a parenting programme had increased the capacity of parents to listen to their children. Parents in a number of studies stated that they had increased the time that they spent listening to their children each day, and that parent–child communication had improved as a consequence of this:

> 'I learned how important listening is. Just listening to my children and finding out they have feelings too. It can't always be "my way or no way". And that's how I used to want it. Now, it's like, let's talk this through and work it out.'
> *(Wolfe 1997, p.96 [Traditional, African-American])*

> 'I listen more effectively and allow the children to work out their problems to a greater extent.'
> *(Gordon-Rosen, 1982, p.113 [Traditional, African-American])*

One of the benefits of an increased capacity to listen to their children was that parents had the opportunity to learn about their children's lives:

> 'If we keep communication open with our children, most likely they will bring their ideas to you. And we will have a chance to learn about, their thinking, their questions, and their play. We can also keep track of their development.'
> *(Yuen, 1997, p.86 [Translated, Chinese])*

Some parents were also aware of the benefits of their improved listening as regards their children's developing sense of independence and autonomy:

> 'My daughter reminded me that I have a choice between going or not going back to Hong Kong. I guess she has picked up what I always say to her during the special playtime. She sounds more autonomous and independent.'
> *(Yuen, 1997, p.92 [Translated, Chinese])*

In addition to improved listening skills, some parents also commented on the changes in the way in which they talked to their children including the way in which they treated their children with increased respect, and allowed proper discussion as opposed to telling their children what to do:

> 'I learned to talk with, rather than at the children.'
> *(Gordon-Rosen, 1982, p.113 [Traditional, African-American])*

Some parents indicated that they had also started praising their children:

'I've found that the effective praise method sends a message to children about parents because they sort of fit with the kind of parent to be, how I could become a better parent. The best thing about effective praise method is that it makes you realise what a good kid you have.'
(Thomas, 2000, p.136, [Culturally Specific, African-American])

Spending more time together

Related to the above theme was that of 'spending more time together':

'Before I started taking the parenting program, I used to go home and leave my son with my mom, and now I spend time, me and him. At first, he wasn't doing well but now he's doing real good.'
(Norwood and others, 1997, p.424 [Culturally Specific, African-American])

Some parents increased the time spent with their children in specific activities such as reading:

'I really feel intimate with my daughter … Every night I am so excited to hug her and read her stories before she goes to sleep.'
(Yuen, 1997, p.88 [Translated, Chinese])

The increase in time spent together was, in a number of cases, directly due to some of the specific techniques taught on some of the parenting programmes such as 'Alone Dates' and 'Chit-Chat time':

'I have started the "alone dates" with my older child. I realise he needs to feel special too … Maybe we would go to dinner, maybe we would take a walk, but always it would be something where we would not be interrupted, where we would have a chance to talk and I would really listen. It was time that was really valued on both sides.'
(Yuen, 1997, pp.86–7 [Translated, Chinese])

Some parenting programmes also appeared to have made an impact on the physical relationship between parent and child, in particular the increased expression of love, and use of physical touch:

'Also physically doing the hugs and touching them and jumping up and down with them or whatever for something that they were proud of doing – it has been a positive effect on them.'
(Thomas, 2000, p.134 [Culturally Specific, African-American])

Some mothers tried to encourage their partner to spend more time with their children:

> 'I encouraged my husband to spend some time to play with the
> children. He is willing to take my suggestion and immediately
> sees the positive impact on their relationship. He learned that
> the children need to build a sense of trust and connection with
> him.'
> *(Yuen 1997, p.87 [Translated, Chinese])*

In some cases the increased time spent with the children had resulted in increased feelings of being valued and wanted on the part of the parent:

> 'I always thought that he only wanted his father. We became more
> distant as he got older. But we enjoyed the playtime so much. He
> acted like a little boy and enjoyed so much my attention in the
> special playtime. I thought that he did not care for my attention
> any more. Now, he will even stop playing computer games for the
> special playtime. I feel like I have my son back.'
> *(Chau, 1996, p.85 [Translated, Chinese])*

Allowing children more freedom

Participation in a parenting programme had resulted in some parents allowing their children a greater amount of autonomy and freedom:

> 'I am an overprotective mother. I thought the way to show I am a
> good parent is to do things for my child, but I overdo it ... I offer
> help that is not necessary. I decide when he is warm and when is
> cold. Now, I remind myself not to be so imposing.'
> *(Yuen, 1997, p.90 [Translated, Chinese])*

Some parents felt that this increase in autonomy and freedom had led to an increase in their children's self-confidence:

> 'My son has always been timid, withdrawn and quiet since he
> came to America I do feel guilty and sorry for him. I thought I
> was helping him. Actually I was stopping him from trying. I took
> away his opportunities for developing himself. He was so happy
> in the playtime that he tried different things without my
> suggestions. He looked so satisfied and confident when he could
> choose what to do and how to do...'
> *(Chau, 1996, p.79 [Translated, Chinese])*

Cox (2002) provides an example of how increased autonomy and independence had helped to bring grandparents and grandchildren closer together:

> '…In one assignment, Mrs G a 75-year-old grandmother
> discussed the use of condoms with her 17-year-old grandson. She
> told him to be sure to use them, to be sure that they were latex,
> and not to keep them in his back pocket where the heat could
> damage them. She reported that after his initial shock, he said,
> "Grandma, you are really pretty cool."'
> *(Cox, 2002, p.49 [Traditional, African-American])*

In addition to increased autonomy and independence, some parents were allowing their children to express their feelings. This was especially true in the case of some Chinese parents:

> 'Although it is still natural for me to have negative feelings when
> my son is fussy, I am more able to accept the fact he also has a
> low mood. I am learning to accept what he is, not just the one
> who can meet my expectations.'
> *(Yuen, 1997, p.90 [Translated, Chinese])*

Increased empathy

Parenting programmes also appeared to have increased empathy, in particular by helping parents to recognise that children have feelings like themselves:

> 'Cause I realised that, even though they might be small, they
> have frustrations and they can be depressed just as much as me.
> And, like you said, they have anger they need to display
> somewhere. And sometime they come home and just let it all
> out. You think they're being mean. I really think my son be really
> aggravating, but I know he's having a hard time at school … I
> just know that they have problems, too, and I just have to realise
> that and try to like help them. And just listen and let them get it
> all out. But it's hard sometimes. They can be so aggravating.'
> *(Wolfe, 1997, pp.96–7 [Traditional, African-American])*

The increased respect for children's feelings and increased autonomy appeared to have resulted in greater cooperation on the part of children, and reduced conflict between parent and child.

Positive discipline

One of the areas in which parenting programmes appeared to be highly successful was changing parents' attitudes toward the use of physical discipline:

> 'My thought now is that you don't have to spank or hit. Using the
> method of talking to your children finding out why would you
> want to feel like you have to hit them. But not, I have learned
> not to hit – I don't like to be hit and so, I try hard not hit them. I
> do sit them down and talk to them when I'm calm and try to find
> out what's really happening, what's really going on.'
> *(Thomas, 2000, p.133 [Culturally Specific, African-American])*

Some parents felt that the parenting programme had helped them to find alternative ways of disciplining their children:

> '…You learn more ways of how to do things, as opposed to doing
> things just one way. Like, you learn how to play in more than one
> way and you learn how to discipline in more than one way. I have
> more than one way to do things now. So if one thing doesn't
> work, I try the other.'
> *(Wolfe, 1997, p.98 [Traditional, African-American]*

The setting of family rules was a technique that many parents found helpful:

> 'If you don't give a child family rules, just family whether you're
> to me, a single parent, because I am or not, what structure are
> you gonna give your children and it's hard to me, I think family
> rules are important and it is a big part of parenting.'
> *(Thomas, 2000, p.137 [Culturally Specific, African-American])*

Atmosphere at home and family relations

In addition to changes in parents and children, there were also changes in the home environment. Parents described how the programme had lead to an improvement in family relations, and improved the atmosphere in the home:

> 'I have established more mutual respect in the family.'
> *(Gordon-Rosen, 1982, p.114 [Traditional, African-American])*

> 'We've been able to reduce the amount of arguing in our family.'
> *(Gordon-Rosen, 1982, p.114 [Traditional, African-American])*

Aspects of parenting programmes that parents found helpful

Approach of the facilitators

The approach of the programme facilitators appears to play an important role in determining how minority ethnic parents experienced a particular programme. Non-judgemental attitudes were particularly important to many parents:

> 'I would say that I thought that you were a good instructor and that you listened to us. You didn't try to judge us in one way or the other. And I made a lot of friends and learned a lot about how they do things at home and what I could do different or what they could do different by learning from me.'
> *(Wolfe, 1997, p.100 [Traditional, African-American])*

Parents liked the fact that they were not made to feel that they were bad parents or that there were 'right' and 'wrong' ways of doing things:

> 'I liked that we weren't told what was wrong so much about what we did, but given positive ideas to help make us better parents.'
> *(Akinyela, 1996, p.233 [Culturally Specific, African-American])*

In addition to not being judged, many parents also valued the fact that the facilitators were 'human' in their approach:

> 'You [the facilitators] made yourselves human and didn't try to act as if you didn't have problems too.'
> *(Akinyela, 1996, p.237 [Culturally Specific, African-American])*

Some of the programmes appear to have provided parents with the opportunity to share experiences with other parents. This may be especially important to parents who do not find this easy or who do not have the opportunity to share their experiences with others:

> '[My best experience was] getting to see how I could talk among the whole group. Cause I'm not really a talkative person, especially about things going on at the house. But to see all them open up, it made it a little easier to talk to them. And to see you, you know, even though you were the leader, tell experiences from your own home. It made it easier for me to talk.'
> *(Wolfe, 1997, p.100 [Traditional, African-American])*

Support provided by the group

In addition to the importance attached by parents to the attitude and approach of the facilitator, parents also appeared to value the support provided by other parents taking part in the programme. Some parents had recognised for the first time that they were not the only ones experiencing particular problems:

> 'What I liked was the fact that I didn't feel alone. I didn't feel like I was the only one going through the situation. I wasn't by myself.'
> *(Thomas, 2000, p.128 [Culturally Specific, African-American])*

Chinese parents participating in a Filial Therapy parenting programme expressed a similar view about the other parents in the group:

> 'I always thought that I was the only one having problems with my son, and that my son was the only one who would be so mean to the parent. It felt really comforting to know that other kids said mean things to the parents, and that other parents have problems too.'
> *(Chau, 1996, p.85 [Translated, Chinese])*

Some of the parenting groups appeared to have provided parents with the opportunity to share deep-seated feelings and problems:

> 'Actually, I think about the class every day because that was like the biggest experience in my life, as far as sharing with other parents since I've been a parent.'
> *(Wolfe, 1997, p.94 [Traditional, African-American])*

Some participants felt that talking to other parents helped them to understand or get a clearer picture of some of the techniques being taught on the programme. In a number of cases the supportive relationships that were established continued beyond the end of the programme, and it is clear that friendships were formed in at least two programmes:

> 'I know that I found a new friend ... Before when I came [to the nursery playscheme] I would drop my son off ... leave and come back to get him ... but I found a friend there we often talk about the programme ... and discuss how we wish they would start the programme back up.'
> *(Akinyela, 1996, p.237 [Culturally Specific, African-American])*

A number of the culturally specific parenting programmes encouraged parents to think of themselves as a 'family', and this lead to increased support for one another (Brave Heart 1999).

> 'We became a family here. I think that was part of the magic that developed in the training, we became empowered ... [the Seven Laws] helped us to be supportive of each other ... grow closer. We really are a family.'
> *(Brave Heart, 1999, p.122 [Culturally Specific, Native American, Lakota])*

Aspects of parenting programmes that parents found unhelpful

In addition to experiencing benefits, parents identified a number of difficulties with parenting programmes some of which focused on conflicts about time and work, and conflicts surrounding childcare. Some parents also experienced difficulties with the methods/techniques being used on the parenting programme, and in maintaining the new skills that they had learned.

Conflicts in relation to time and work

Some parents experienced conflicting feelings about attending a parenting programme because of other time commitments. This affected their ability to attend sessions. The most commonly cited reason for not attending sessions was that of finding the time to attend, because of work commitments in particular:

> 'Just the logistics and it's not an excuse, it's just the logistics of you get off from work, you've gotta feed your kids, otherwise they're gonna be bouncing off the wall if you have to bring them here, or you've got to make sure they're settled in at home, before you can come here and focus on the class. And, I think that was sometimes challenging for a lot of folks in all groups – it didn't always allow us to start when we wanted to, or cancel our classes.'
> *(Thomas, 2000, p.142 [Culturally Specific, African-American])*

Conflicts about childcare

Another key conflict in terms of participating in a parenting programme was the provision of childcare. Whilst some parenting programmes provided crèche facilities, in a number of cases parents had to arrange their own childcare. Some parents had to rely on relatives, and one mother relied on her grandmother:

> 'For myself, as I say I live with my grandmother also. And, she's the one that usually cares for my kids if I have classes or meetings or whatever, and sometimes she just really wouldn't be – she hasn't been feeling that good, so sometimes when she's not feeling good, I felt I couldn't just leave them, but then it's only one care giver here during the meeting, I felt bad to bring them. So, it's like, "Okay, I'll just stay home, I'll pick it up next time, or something like that."'
>
> *(Thomas, 2000, pp.142–3 [Culturally Specific, African-American])*

Many women also relied on their husbands for childcare, which meant that they had to attend the programme without their partner:

> 'My husband does do some and we do trade off, and I'm usually good with the Boy Scouts thing and sometimes I'll ask him to go and take them for me. But he will – I work – I can work late and stay at work five [o'clock], I might be there until six. So he is there to cover that gap from three to six.'
>
> *(Thomas, 2000, p.143 [Culturally Specific, African-American])*

Methods of delivering the programme

There were also strong feelings about the methods used in the parenting programmes. Perhaps of most interest is the fact that some parents' views about particular methods appear to have changed over the course of the programme. For example, in one study the participating grandparents experienced considerable trepidation about the use of role-play. However, as the programme progressed, Cox reports that many participating parents found that this technique helped relieve the tension around difficult issues (Cox, 2002, [Traditional, African-American]). Similarly, many grandparents taking part in this study had dreaded giving presentations, but having completed the presentation found it to be one of the most rewarding aspects of the programme (ibid.).

However, some parents' views had not changed by the end of the programme, and in some cases, parents did not understand the meaning or purpose of particular techniques that were used:

> 'The meditation was different because I didn't understand that.'
> *(Akinyela, 1996, p.237 [Culturally Specific, African-American])*

There was also evidence to suggest that parents within the same group could have very different experiences of the same technique, which is demonstrated by the following two quotations:

> 'The highlight of the Circle to me was the mirror exercise. That was the most important. I like to get deep.'
> *(Akinyela, 1996, p.233 [Culturally Specific, African-American])*

> 'I found the mirror exercise difficult also, because I was always getting put down by other people.'
> *(Akinyela, 1996, p.237 [Culturally Specific, African-American])*

Some parents found that the discussion provoked strong feelings:

> 'Some of the discussion questions provoked inappropriately intense discussion among parents and that some discussion questions should be modified or "watered down" so that parents do not take issues personally, become angry with each other, and upset the group.'
> *(Day, 1995, p.157 [Traditional, African-American])*

Parenting techniques

While parents felt overall that they had new tools with which to manage their children's difficult behaviour, some parents also expressed uncertainty or difficulty in applying the techniques being taught:

> 'Ignoring method. I don't quite understand how you can just ignore your kid or anybody.'
> *(Thomas, 2000, p.139 [Culturally Specific, African-American])*

One mother indicated that part of her difficulty in using 'ignoring' related to her partner's ways of parenting:

'Basically, the ignoring method didn't work for me, because I
think they were too far gone in our relationship to – for him to
even think that was happening. The difficulty with it for me,
things that I've felt should be ignored "Daddy didn't" and things
that I felt should be dealt with, Daddy felt should be ignored. So,
it wasn't the method that didn't work, but you have to have a
certain level of preparation before you even decide [laughter].'
(Thomas, 2000, p.139 [Culturally Specific, African-American])

Other parents found family rules difficult to implement. One mother described how
it can be difficult implementing such rules within different family structures:

'One of the difficulties in a parenting class is that one parent is
learning and another already knows or thinks he knows [laugh]
that or whatever and parents have differing perceptions of what
the family rules are and what the limits are and those things tend
to very – it gets more complicated. So that's one of the things
that we realised we should have worked out before we started.'
(Thomas, 2000, p.140 [Culturally Specific, African-American])

In one particular study, many parents appeared to dislike the use of points and
charts:

'I do not like the point system and I don't like charting.'
(Thomas, 2000, p.140 [Culturally Specific, African-American])

Maintaining new skills

While many parents developed new skills as a result of taking part in a parenting
programme, there was some evidence to suggest that parents also experienced
difficulties in maintaining the newly learned skills once the programme was over.
One of the main problems identified was finding time to continue using their skills:

'I came home very late at around 11 p.m. She was waiting for me
to have the special playtime. I was so exhausted and wanted to
say "No". But I did not want to disappoint her and felt good that
she was so eager to spend time with me. Once we started, I was
not tired anymore. Even though I did not say much, she just
loved me being there. And I enjoyed seeing her play.'
(Chau, 1996, p.77 [Translated, Chinese])

Comparison with other qualitative studies

The findings of these qualitative studies about the experiences of minority ethnic parents who have taken part in a parenting programme mirror many of the findings about white parents who have taken part in such programmes (e.g. Barlow and Stewart-Brown, 2001). Both minority ethnic and white parents identified similar benefits in terms of more positive discipline, increased empathy, spending more time together, feeling less stressed and more in control, and better communications with their children. There are also similarities in terms of parents' motivations for taking part, their feelings of being supported by group facilitators and the benefits of being in a group with other parents.

Summary

- Parents from diverse minority ethnic groups including African-American, Chinese, and Native American, reported experiencing a range of benefits as a result of taking part in a parenting programme.

- Parents appeared to benefit from both traditional and culturally specific parenting programmes and from behavioural and relationship programmes.

- Not all of the benefits reported, however, will have accrued to all the parents in all the programmes and the findings are based on data from parents who completed programmes and do not represent the views of the dissatisfied minority who dropped out of programmes prematurely (i.e. before the programme was completed).

- Parents found the skills of the facilitators to be important in helping them adapt their parenting skills. They also valued the support of other parents in the group. Many parents reported having expressed their feelings and concerns for the first time, and having experienced relief and support as a result of realising they were not the only parent experiencing difficulties. In a number of cases, the support from other parents continued beyond the end of the parenting programme.

- While many of the parents who were mandated to attend parenting programmes were resentful at the outset, such feelings changed as the programme progressed, with many participants reporting positively about the programme.

- Some parents reported difficulties in attending the parenting programme as a result of work and other commitments, in addition to having problems with childcare. Parents also talked about the difficulties of maintaining new skills beyond the duration of the programme, and of not liking some aspect of programmes.

- The experiences of minority ethnic parents reported in these studies are in many respects very similar to the experiences of white parents who have taken part in parenting programmes.

Culturally specific and traditional programmes

The results of the qualitative studies provide clear testimony to the success of both traditional and culturally sensitive parenting programmes in supporting parents and in helping them to find alternative, more helpful ways of encouraging children's social and emotional development. Many working in this field, however, remain concerned about the issue of cultural sensitivity, and in particular, whether traditional parenting programmes take into account the values of minority ethnic parents. The remainder of this chapter explores some of the issues surrounding culture and parenting programmes by comparing the different experiences of parents who take part in traditional and culturally specific parenting programmes.

Values and parenting programmes

The majority of 'traditional' parenting programmes are designed and delivered by white, middle-class individuals. They have, more specifically, mostly been designed to meet the needs of white, British, European and American parents. Traditional parenting programmes are therefore mostly based on the values of dominant cultures as opposed to the values of minority ethnic groups. One of the concerns of many working in the field is that parenting programmes may fail to reflect, and thereby fail to respect, the values and traditions of parents from different ethnic groups; or even more problematic, that they may recommend practices that actually conflict with the culture and traditions of ethnic minority participants. Traditional parenting programmes may not only lack cultural sensitivity in terms of their failure to endorse the values of the participating parents, they may also be regarded as continuing a tradition in which white imperialists impose their values and culture on supposedly more primitive groups of people. One parent who took part in a culturally specific parenting programme expressed this issue very clearly:

> 'I expected it to be like the "Peach program" where there was a
> group of women and a white lady telling us how to be.'
> *(Akinyela, 1996, p.232 [Culturally Specific, Native American])*

Other minority ethnic parents also expressed concern at the outset that they might
be expected to conform to the values of the dominant culture. For example, Chau
(1996) found that Chinese parents were very sceptical at the start of a traditional
(translated) parenting programme about the special playtime sessions, and more
importantly that they would have to express their emotions far more than their
culture normally required:

> 'I am afraid what we have to do here is to say "Honey,
> Sweetheart, Sugar … I love you" like what the Americans do. But
> we're just not this way.'
> *(Chau, 1996, p.79 [Translated, Chinese])*

The incompatibility between the values underpinning parenting programmes, and
those of the participating parents, may be so extensive that it is difficult to convey
the meaning or value of some components being taught on the programme. This
was demonstrated by the following remarks by a Chinese parent who had taken part
in a traditional (Translated) parenting programme (Filial Therapy):

> 'The concepts of love and affection are seldom discussed in
> Chinese culture. When questions were translated, it was difficult
> to match the vocabulary with the concept. The investigator had
> to use additional phrases and examples to express [the] idea of
> affection. Even when the parents understood the words, it was
> more difficult for them to identify with the idea of affection…'
> *(Chau, 1996, p.81 [Translated, Chinese])*

The next section of this chapter compares the experiences of parents who take part
in traditional, compared with culturally specific, parenting programmes, focusing in
particular on what happens when the values underpinning a parenting programme
conflict with the values of the participating parents.

When values conflict

The relationship between parenting practices and culture was explored in an earlier section (see Chapter 2), where it was concluded that parenting practices are informed by the culture of different ethnic groups. This was particularly apparent with Asian-American parents, and to a lesser extent African-American parents (see below). For example, it has been suggested that Chinese parenting practices have been influenced in particular by Confucianism with a resulting emphasis on parents' control, obedience, strict discipline, filial piety, respect for elders, family obligations, maintenance of harmony, and negation of conflict (Lin and Fu, 1990, in Chau and Landreth, 1997).

Many traditional parenting programmes, however, recommend parenting practices that are in direct conflict with such values. For example, one of the filial parenting programmes recommended that participating Chinese parents encourage and help their children to express negative and difficult feelings. This is in contrast with traditional Chinese culture, which has been characterised as recommending the punishment of children who express difficult or non-harmonious feelings.

When the values underpinning a parenting programme are in conflict with the values of the participating parents, one of two outcomes may occur. First, there is considerable scope for the breakdown of relationships, including non-attendance and drop out. Alternatively, the parents may adapt their parenting to match the values being advocated. There was some evidence of the latter in the case of Chinese parents, who had participated in a traditional parenting programme in which some of their core cultural values were being challenged. This is indicated by the following two quotations from Chinese parents who had participated in a traditional filial therapy parenting programme:

> 'Whenever she was jealous of her brother or had a fight with
> him, I would scold her, stop her from expressing her anger or
> explain to her how wrong it was. I was afraid that accepting those
> feelings might increase the intensity and frequency. After starting
> filial training I tried to accept and reflect her jealousy in the
> playtime and daily life. It is interesting that she used to complain
> that I had not been fair. She does not complain as often now. But
> I had not really changed the way I treated the two of them.
> Maybe accepting her feelings was important.'
> *(Chau, 1996, p.81 [Translated, Chinese])*

> 'I used to discourage or even stop my children from crying. I was
> hoping to make them stronger. After this class, I am able to put
> myself into his shoes and reflect his feelings. He even calms
> down faster than he used to and we feel closer.'
> *(Chau, 1996, p.81 [Translated, Chinese])*

Participation in a Filial Therapy parenting programme also appeared to have
resulted in the following parent reflecting on the way in which she herself had been
parented, and using new parenting practices:

> 'I just use the same way my parents raised me because I did not
> know another way. I never thought that parents should
> communicate acceptance to their children. When my son said
> hateful things to me, I felt hurt and angry. Immediately wanted
> to stop and punish him. Now I try to reflect and accept his anger
> like what we have learned. He's showing less frustration and
> anger toward me lately. I think our relationship is getting better.
> Sometimes, he come to hug me and says that he loves me. I feel
> so close with my son. My husband also notice the changes.'
> *(Chau, 1996, p.80 [Translated, Chinese])*

Despite the fact that this Filial Therapy parenting programme had challenged
traditional Chinese views about children's autonomy, this particular parent had
nevertheless taken on board the new practices being recommended:

> 'I never thought that children need to be respected for their
> autonomy. I was afraid that they would become disobedient. But
> when I respect his autonomy more, he seems to be more
> cooperative. We have less power struggles then.'
> *(Chau, 1996, p.82 [Translated, Chinese])*

Overall, these results suggest that while many Chinese-American parents were
sceptical at the outset about some of the parenting practices being recommended –
perhaps most importantly those that challenged traditional practices based on
culture – many nevertheless adopted the new practices. In a number of cases,
parents reported positive outcomes in terms of their children's happiness or
adjustment. This is demonstrated by the following quotation from a father who had
been taught the importance of play:

> 'I always do something educational with my son. I used to believe
> that I should teach my son something, all the time I did not see any
> reason for just playing together with him. The play time is really
> special for us, I realise that my son needs to have fun with me.'
> *(Chau, 1996, p.77 [Translated, Chinese])*

The findings from these Chinese-American parents suggest that traditional parenting programmes may be functioning to reconcile minority ethnic parents with aspects of the dominant culture, or more specifically their children's bi-cultural identity. While the appropriateness of this process of 'assimilation' might be questioned, some of these changes appear to have been beneficial as regards parent–child relationships, and children's well-being. This was demonstrated by one father's changing views concerning his daughter's role in society. At the outset, he expressed the following beliefs:

> 'Girls should be quiet and help with housework at home. I don't
> understand why she always acts like a boy. She always plays boy
> stuff. She acts abnormal. Sometimes, I feel ashamed of her.'
> *(Chau, 1996, p.83 [Translated, Chinese])*

In a later session, however, his views had altered slightly:

> 'I knew she would play with that dart gun. I thought about hiding
> it. But I did let her play with it. In fact, we had fun playing together.
> But I can't stop myself hoping she would be like other girls.'
> *(Chau, 1996, p.83 [Translated, Chinese])*

Another Chinese-American father who had taken part in a parenting programme had also experienced challenges to his cultural beliefs about the role of girls and women in society. Participation in the programme had enabled him to begin to think about and accept the changed cultural environment in which he was living, with a positive outcome for his daughter:

> 'Maybe it is not that bad for a girl to play soccer after all. There
> really is nothing wrong with soccer. Time has changed and the
> world has changed. I just let her decide, and she seemed so happy.'
> *(Chau, 1996, p.87 [Translated, Chinese])*

The findings of this study also indicate, however, that the challenging of traditional values can leave parents feeling distressed or sad. One Chinese-American parent who had taken part in a traditional Filial Therapy parenting programme explained:

> 'I have been listening to my parents' opinions all my life. They
> made most of the decisions for me including my marriage. It was
> tough. Now as a mother, I have to learn to follow my son's lead.
> When will it be my turn to lead? But I don't want him to wait
> until my age to learn how to make decisions.'
> *(Chau, 1996, p.78 [Translated, Chinese])*

While feelings of conflict might ultimately lead to positive change, if these feelings
are not recognised by programme facilitators and parents provided with appropriate
support they may lead to less positive outcomes including conflict within the family,
and drop out from the programme. The drop-out rate from parenting programmes
can be as high as 50 per cent, and in the case of minority ethnic parents this may
reflect the mismatch between their values and those being advocated by the
programme.

While traditional parenting programmes may be underpinned by values that are
different to those of the participating parents, culturally specific parenting
programmes may also be based on values that are in conflict with those of the
participating parents. For example, the Effective Black Parenting Programme
(EBPP) incorporates units that specifically aim to help black parents to understand
the historical and cultural reasons for what is described as 'the use of physical
discipline within black culture', whilst also challenging its use and helping parents to
develop different methods of discipline. This is demonstrated by the following two
quotations from African-American parents whose values concerning discipline were
challenged by the parenting programme:

> 'Spanking is a very difficult subject. What I appreciated coming
> away from the class was the historical reasoning for African
> Americans surrounding spanking and hitting and discipline. Your
> child could be killed if they're acting out in the wrong place. So,
> they were spanked or hit or whipped to save their lives, pretty
> much and culturally, that's been handed down.'
> *(Thomas, 2000, p.134 [Culturally Specific, African-American])*

> 'The reasons for the not spanking piece really hits (sic) home
> when you realise the historical perspective of why we go back to
> that, and most of us would probably spank.'
> *(Thomas, 2000, p.134 [Culturally Specific, African-American])*

The results of this study suggest that both traditional and culturally specific parenting programmes may be underpinned by values that conflict with (or are different from) those of the parents. This issue is not, however, unique to parents of minority ethnic groups. Physical punishment and spanking are important issues for many white parents, and are often underpinned by religious or cultural beliefs. In the studies reviewed the conflict of values between those of the programme providers and those of the participating parents often seemed to result in positive outcomes. The findings of this review suggest, however, that there are a number of important differences between traditional and culturally specific parenting programmes as regards this 'conflict of values'. First, and perhaps most importantly, it seems likely that the potential discrepancy of values is frequently not recognised or acknowledged by traditional programme facilitators, and that this 'clash of values' may therefore occur without the preparation or forethought of programme providers and without the necessary preparation in terms of addressing the feelings of participating parents. The developers and facilitators of culturally specific parenting programmes, however, have paid considerable attention to the possibility of conflicting values such as, for example, the conflict that was anticipated in the Effective Black Parenting Programmes as regards the issue of discipline. In this particular case, careful attention was given to helping parents to address the conflict by locating current parenting values and practices within the particular historical and cultural history of black people. This not only enabled parents to understand the historical context of their current practices, but to move on to new methods of discipline based on what is described as being the changed position of black people within modern society.

Second, the largely positive response on the part of respondents in this review was obtained from a small and unrepresentative minority ethnic group – Chinese parents who had taken part in a traditional Filial Therapy parenting programme. In this case the programme was provided by Chinese facilitators, who would have been aware of the potential clash of values, and who may have taken appropriate steps to address the needs of the participating parents. In addition to this, it has been suggested that Chinese culture places great emphasis on diligence and obedience. If this is the case, it may have played a significant role in determining the response of the participating parents to the overt challenge to their value system. Parents from other minority ethnic groups who are not imbued with such a strong sense of obedience and discipline might adopt a more challenging stance, including dropping out of the programme.

Providing a positive view about culture

In addition to challenging parenting practices, one of the most important themes to emerge from the interviews with parents who had taken part in a culturally specific parenting programme was the way in which the programme had provided them with a positive view of their own culture. In some cases, the programme had helped parents to develop a new awareness of aspects of their culture. This suggests that parenting programmes may not only have a role to play in challenging traditional practices, but also in raising awareness and endorsing positive aspects of different cultures. This is demonstrated by the following quotation provided by Native Americans from the Lakota tribe who had taken part in a culturally specific parenting programme:

> 'My favourite stuff is the Seven Laws of the Lakota because when we discussed this we didn't know these laws and we're all Lakota. We want everyone to know these laws. We wanted to put up posters … What stuck in my mind is that if we live by these laws then everything would be different, we'd all be living in harmony. To me, that's the traditional way to live … so Lakota families can be born and raised with our own Lakota values … And be the strong Lakota nation that we're supposed to be.'
> *(Brave Heart, 1999, p.121 [Culturally Specific, Native Americans, Lakota])*

Similarly, the Effective Black Parenting Programme comprises a number of units that are aimed at encouraging black parents to be proud of being black, and to help their children be proud of their cultural heritage. Parents are encouraged to expose their children to positive images of black people and black culture, and to avoid 'black put-downs':

> 'The Pride in Blackness piece and the things that we need to do either very overtly or subtlety, to make our children or expose our children to … To expose them to black folks doing positive things and making sure that they see or see the balance … I agree that more needs to be put in the Pride in Blackness and avoiding black put-downs.'
> *(Thomas, 2000, p.138 [Culturally Specific])*

These findings also indicate, however, that the use of new practices by parents was not without problems. One parent described the difficulties in avoiding black put-downs when her daughter was ostracised at school for working hard:

> 'My daughter at a school goes through really bad vibes with the black girls because she goes to school and does what she needs to do. So, the black girls didn't want to play with her. It's been hard for me to do the – like avoid black put-downs and starting blackness and all that.'
> *(Thomas, 2000, p.137 [Culturally Specific])*

Another parent talked about the difficulty in conveying her children's cultural heritage to them:

> 'My boy is a different thing, we're in an area of different races, but when the subject comes up, like about the slavery, talk about slavery and some of the courses, he's ten, and he's like yeah, yeah, yeah. But, I'm gonna keep doing it, and I'm gonna tell him just like I try to tell as many people as I can, "I have a little appreciation of what the slaves went through".'
> *(Thomas, 2000, p.138 [Culturally Specific])*

Other parents pointed to the difficulties in finding positive role models and images for their children:

> 'But, the thing is, they see this – outside … Because, by it being racially mixed, they only see the blacks doing it, they don't see any other races doing it. And, I'm kinda lost on what to say to the guy, television comes in handy, because there's a lot of black folks that's on television that's doing something positive and my son – and I will bring that out to my son, thank goodness for that. But, once we walk out that door, it's an entirely different story, and like the only thing I think I can do is – "you got to make your own mind up on how you want your life to go".'
> *(Thomas, 2000, p.138 [Culturally Specific, African-American])*

In addition to providing parents with a positive view about their own culture, a number of the culturally specific parenting programmes (e.g. Brave Heart, 1999) highlighted ways in which the cultural specificity of the programme enabled parents to understand and move on from some of the traumas that had played a significant role in determining the way in which they were parented. The historical trauma of the Lakota Tribe of Native Americans has been used as a framework for the design of a parenting skills curriculum. One of the goals of this parenting programme was to facilitate parents' awareness of 'life span and communal trauma across generations', in particular by raising parents' consciousness of the way in which previous generations had suffered from the abusive boarding school system:

> 'Lakota people, perhaps parents that lived through the trauma of boarding school are now in a position to really support children, but many don't. Do we know no other way? We need to free ourselves from the trauma.'
> *(Brave Heart, 1999, p.118 [Culturally Specific, Native Americans, Lakota])*

This had enabled the participating parents to understand some of the barriers that their own parents had built and the effects of this on their lives:

> 'My parents never shared anything … [Father] had a lot of shame and anger he carried around with him that I didn't know until I asked and he spilled his guts … I got closer to my dad and I think it helped lessen his load a bit.'
> *(Brave Heart, 1999, p.119 [Culturally Specific, Native Americans, Lakota])*

This process had enabled some parents to move on from blaming their parents in order to concentrate on the needs of their own children:

> 'My role and responsibility to keep the children sacred are to remain patient, to trust, to listen, to assist, and to be a better parent. The big difference now is that I can't blame my parents because they haven't taught me. Now that I know it's my responsibility I know that I'll teach my son and I want my son to teach his children. We can make a better life for the future of our children …'
> *(Brave Heart, 1999, p.119 [Culturally Specific, Native Americans, Lakota])*

A number of parents who took part in culturally sensitive parenting programmes also developed closer relationships with blood relatives as a result of having taken part in the programme. This resulted in part from their ability to share what they had learned in the programme with other members of the family, and from their changed attitudes towards other family members:

'I found myself getting to know my relatives and going out to celebrations. [My kids are] having a good time meeting their grandmothers and grandfathers. I found that being in this program gave me an awareness of how important these relatives are and how important being a part of a community is.'
(Brave Heart, 1999, p.122 [Culturally Specific, Native American])

Summary

- Both traditional and culturally sensitive parenting programmes have a role to play in supporting parents and in challenging unhelpful parenting practices.
- Culturally specific programmes have 'added value' such as, for example, recognition of the fact that parenting programmes may be underpinned by, and promulgate, practices that are based on values that are discrepant with the values of the participating parents.
- Culturally sensitive parenting programmes include methods of supporting parents through the feelings that such challenges to their value system might induce.
- Culturally specific parenting programmes appear to play an important role in enhancing and extending parents' knowledge about their culture, including the role that particular traumas have played in terms of the development of parenting practices, and thereby enabling parents to 'move on' from such traumas.

5. Parenting programmes for minority ethnic parents: what works?

Introduction

This chapter describes the results of the quantitative studies that were identified by the review and has three aims. First, to address whether parenting programmes are effective with parents from different minority ethnic groups. Second, to address whether they are more effective with parents from some ethnic groups than others; and third to address whether culturally sensitive (culturally specific and culturally adapted) parenting programmes are more effective than traditional parenting programmes.

Are parenting programmes effective with minority ethnic parents?

The following sections of this chapter examine the effectiveness of parenting programmes with five minority ethnic groups of parents – Black (mostly African-American), Hispanic, Asian (Chinese and Asian Pacific Islanders living in America and Canada), Native American, and Mixed Race (a mixture of all of the above plus some Latino and white families). The aim of this section is to assess whether different parenting programmes are effective with parents from different ethnic groups. The first part of the chapter focuses on outcomes for children, the second part focuses on outcomes for parents, and the final section focuses on outcomes for families.

The findings of this section are based on a total of 39 studies. A detailed summary of the number of studies evaluating outcomes for each ethnic group, the methodologies used, and the methodological limitations of the studies, is provided in Appendix 2. It should be noted that the discussion that follows does not include the results of the two comparative studies (i.e. the studies that compared outcomes across different ethnic groups – Reid, Webster-Stratton and Beauchaine, 2001 and Steele and others, 2002), as these are discussed in the following section.

The results for individual outcomes from individual studies are presented in the section at the end of the chapter, 'Results of quantitative studies'.

Child outcomes

The included studies measured a range of important child outcomes including emotional and behavioural adjustment, crime, educational attainment, self-concept and play.

Emotional and behavioural adjustment

As with studies of the effectiveness of parenting programmes for white parents, emotional and behavioural adjustment was one of the main outcomes measured in many studies with children from a number of different ethnic groups. Two studies provided evidence concerning the emotional and behavioural adjustment of black children. One study showed that a traditional parenting programme (Interpersonal Cognitive Problem Solving Skills) produced significant improvements in the behaviour of children of black parents who took part in the programme. This improvement included behaviours characteristic of impulsivity (impatience, over-emotionality, aggression) and inhibition (excessive control of feelings or actions). There was also small but non-significant change in concern for others, being liked by peers, autonomy, and in initiative (Tulloch, 1996). A second study examined the effectiveness of the culturally specific Effective Black Parenting Programme (EBPP) in improving the emotional and behavioural adjustment of two cohorts of inner-city African-American children. The results showed significant reductions in behavioural withdrawal and hyperactivity in boys receiving treatment, and in sexual problems in girls in the first cohort. A second cohort showed significant improvements in delinquent behaviours in both girls and boys, and in the social competence of girls (Myers and others, 1992).

There was also evidence to show that parenting programmes can impact on the emotional and behavioural adjustment of Hispanic children. There was a small but non-significant fall in the number of disciplinary referrals in a group of fourth-grade Spanish children whose parents had taken part in a culturally adapted Systematic Training for Parenting Programme (STEP), compared with the number of disciplinary referrals in the control group (Davis, 1994). There were also improvements in both distractibility and hyperactivity for Hispanic children receiving special education preschool services whose parents took part in one of two traditional parenting programmes (Rational Emotive Behaviour Therapy (REBT) and a standard behavioural management programme) (Perez-Nieves, 2001). There was, however, no improvement in attention problems for the behavioural group (ibid.). There was also evidence of large, significant improvements in parent assessments of children's behaviour following participation in a culturally adapted version of the STEP Programme (Villegas, 1977).

There was evidence of effectiveness for ethnically mixed groups, one study showing significant improvement in some measures of ethnically mixed parents' (African-American, Latino, White, Mixed) perceptions of children's behaviour following participation in the traditional STAR programme (Nicholson and others, 2002). Overall, however, there were no improvements in independent observations of outcome and only two out of nine measures of behaviour showed significant improvement.

The effectiveness of a translated version of the SOS – Help for Parents programme in improving child outcomes for three groups of ethnically mixed children was also evaluated (African-American and Latino) – those with clinical emotional and behavioural problems, a non-clinical group, and a control group (Tulloch, 1996). The results showed that there were large but non-significant improvements in conduct, impulsive-hyperactivity, psychosomatic symptoms, anxiety and hyperactivity for the clinical group of children compared with the non-clinical group and the control group. There were a number of modest improvements for the non-clinical group.

There was also evidence, however, to suggest that some parenting programmes did not impact on the emotional well-being or behaviour of minority ethnic children. One study showed that there were no significant differences between the intervention and control group as regards behaviour or the number of absences/lateness of black inner-city junior high-school students, following their parents' participation in a traditional parenting programme (Adlerian and STEP combined) (Gordon-Rosen and Rosen, 1984). The reason for the failure of this study to identify any significant changes in children's emotional and behavioural adjustment may be twofold. First, the numbers were small and may not have been large enough to detect significant differences. Second, there is evidence to indicate that Adlerian and STEP programmes may not be as effective as behavioural programmes in improving behavioural outcomes, irrespective of the ethnicity of the participating parents (Todres and Bunston, 1993). Pitts (2001) showed no improvements in parents' perceptions of children's emotional and behavioural adjustment following participation in a modified version of the Effective Black

Parenting Programme compared with a control group. There were also no significant differences between the two groups in teacher ratings of behaviour. This result may be due in part to the fact that this study evaluated a considerably modified version of the EBPP.

Similarly, while a further study showed a significant improvement in the emotionality/tension of black children aged 7 to 18 years following their foster parents' participation in a traditional parenting programme (Systematic Skills Training), there were once again no significant improvements in non-conformism, self-disclosure, self-esteem, or the stability of the foster placement (Levant and Slattery, 1982). The authors hypothesise that the reasons for the absence of effect on emotional and behavioural adjustment in this study may reflect the fact that the programme did not impact on the foster parents themselves or their communication skills, that the programme was too ambitious for the time allowed, and that the sample was drawn from an urban poor population. Many participants had considerable life stresses that encroached on class time and interfered with the planned course of instruction (ibid.). This study suggests that impoverished foster parents may need more sustained support compared with birth parents.

Crime

One study provided evidence to show that parenting programmes can have an impact on crime rates. Parker-Scott (1999) compared the arrest rates in ethnically mixed groups (African-American, Hispanic and Asian parents) who had taken part in a range of parenting programmes (not named). The results showed that there was a reduction in the six-month re-arrest rate of male adolescents (aged 13–17 years) whose parents had participated in a parenting programme compared with adolescents whose parents had not taken part in such a programme. However, the results of this retrospective study should be treated with caution.

Academic Performance

A number of studies showed that parenting programmes can be effective in improving academic performance. One study showed an improvement in IQ following participation in a Mothers' Discussion Group (Slaughter, 1983), and a further study showed a significant impact on the reading and maths scores of low-income inner-city African-American children compared with children in the control group following participation in a culturally specific parenting programme (Norwood and others, 1997). A third study showed a large but non-significant improvement in the learning problems of an ethnically mixed clinical group of children, compared with a non-clinical group and a control group, following participation in a translated version of the SOS programme (Tulloch, 1996). However, there was also evidence from one study to show that despite a significant improvement in language and in overall attitude toward school, there was no significant improvement in either reading or maths scores in a group of fourth-grade Spanish children whose parents had taken part in a culturally adapted STEP programme (Davis, 1994).

Self-concept and moral reasoning

Educational interventions have been used with varying degrees of success to improve children's moral reasoning and self-concept. There was, however, no evidence to support the use of parenting programmes to improve either of these outcomes in black children (Pembroke, 1980). It should be noted that the one study that measured these outcomes had small numbers (i.e. less than 30 in each arm) and that the programme was delivered by a white facilitator, which may have played an important part in influencing parents' attitudes toward the intervention. The authors hypothesise that the poor finding may also be due to the fact that parents' verbal behaviour but not their attitudes changed as a result of the parenting programme. In addition, self-concept is a complex construct comprising many elements (i.e. esteem; social realism; identification with mother, father, teacher; friends; social interest and minority identification), some aspects of which were not measured by the instrument used in this study (e.g. extroversion/introversion and masculinity/femininity, etc.), and it may be that insufficient time was allowed for change in this domain. Finally, it seems likely that other factors in addition to parent attitudes and behaviour (i.e. sibling and peer relations and school achievement) may play an important role in influencing self-concept.

Social competence

Child competence is important to enable children to function well at school and in other environments. There was some evidence to show that parenting programmes (in this case a translated filial therapy programme) were effective in significantly improving child competence (cognitive and physical) and social acceptance (peer and maternal) in Canadian-Chinese children. There was, however, no evidence of any improvement in children's self-perception concerning their achievement or well-being (Yuen, 1997).

Problem solving

There was also evidence to show that traditional parenting programmes in particular (Interpersonal Cognitive Problem Solving Skills Programme) can impact on the ability of black children to problem solve, and more specifically to think of alternative solutions (i.e. to think of different ways that the child could obtain a toy from another child), in addition to their ability to think about the consequences of a particular action (i.e. the effects of grabbing a toy from another child rather than asking). However, there was limited evidence of improvement in children's ability to think of problem solutions and their consequences, or to perceive such problems as being interpersonal (Shure and Spivack, 1978).

Play

Play is now recognised as being important to the well-being of children. Two studies provided evidence to show that a translated parenting programme (Filial Therapy) (Glover and Landreth, 2000), and a Mothers' Discussion Group (Slaughter, 1983) could be effective in improving aspects of play behaviour in Native American children, including the child's self-directiveness.

Parent outcomes

The included studies measured a range of important outcomes for parents including parenting attitudes and behaviour, parenting competence, parental mental health, problem solving and racial identity.

Parent attitudes

A large number of studies measured parenting attitudes. One study showed that a series of translated programmes were effective in significantly improving a range of black parenting behaviours including discipline, helping children with their school work, helping children to develop a positive self-concept, and new ways to talk with children about sex education (Leal, 1985). There were, however, no significant improvements in the extent to which parents felt that they enjoyed doing things with their children, enjoyed being a parent, liked making personal sacrifices to help their children, or looked forward to their children growing more independent. This study did not use random allocation to groups or matching, and undertook an analysis of the post-test results only without any adjustment for pre-test differences or confounders (i.e. did not compare the change in both groups). The results may therefore be flawed. In addition, the significance levels for some of the outcomes that were measured in this study were not reported.

Black parents reported improvements in a number of attitudes, including subtle indicators of rejection such as parents' resentment and shaming, and in one cohort only, hostile/aggressive rejection (e.g. ridicule and corporal punishment) following participation in the EBPP programme (Myers and others, 1992). They also reported that they felt significantly more positive about their relationship with the target child, and in one cohort there were also improvements in parents' warmth and acceptance. Parents were also significantly more likely to use praise, and less likely to use spanking, in one cohort, but not the other. A further study showed that there were significant improvements in the acceptance/rejection of black parents of both preschool and older children who took part in two traditional parenting programmes (Confident Parenting programme and the PET programme), but no improvement for parents who took part in the STEP programme (Alvy, 1988).

There was also evidence of change in the parenting attitudes of Asian parents following participation in a parenting programme. Two studies showed that a translated filial therapy parenting programme was effective in significantly improving a number of parenting attitudes including respect for children's feelings and their right to express them, appreciation of the child's unique make-up, recognition of the child's need for autonomy and independence, and unconditional love (Chau and Landreth, 1997; Yuen, 1997). These two studies showed that a filial parenting programme was effective in significantly improving parent empathy in relation to three aspects of adult–child interactions – communication of acceptance, allowing the child self-direction, and parent involvement.

A Filial Therapy programme also produced a significant improvement in the empathy of Native American parents during parent–child interaction including communication of acceptance, allowing the child self-direction, and involvement (Glover and Landreth, 2000). There was, however, no significant improvement in parent acceptance, respect for the child's feelings and their right to express them, appreciation of the child's unique make-up, recognition of the child's need for autonomy and independence, or unconditional love.

A number of studies showed that some parenting programmes did not impact on the parenting attitudes or behaviour of participating parents. For example, Pembroke (1980) showed that there was no change in the disciplinarian attitudes of black parents who had taken part in a traditional parenting programme. However, only half of the participants returned questionnaires thereby reducing the sample size from 22 to 11 parents. This means that the results cannot be generalised to all parents who took part in the parenting programme and also that the sample may have been too small to identify significant changes (ibid.).

Similarly, Levant and Slobodian (1981) showed that there was no significant improvement in a range of parenting behaviours following a skills-training programme for black foster parents of children aged 7–18 years. The behaviours examined included empathic understanding, facilitative genuineness, respect, acceptance, and structuring. There was also no improvement in parents' acceptance, or the ability of the foster parent and child to discuss, examine and resolve a conflict constructively, or in their use of rules and limit-setting (ibid.). The authors suggest that this lack of impact may be due to the fact that the study was undertaken with a highly stressed urban poor population. The small numbers may also have contributed to the failure to identify significant change.

One study showed negligible improvements for parents of black children in the following parent attitudes – confidence, acceptance, trust or causation following participation in a behavioural parenting programme (SOS! Help for parents) (Tulloch, 1996). There were, however, a number of moderate non-significant improvements for the group of parents with children outside the clinical range including understanding, trust and acceptance.

Creswell-Betsch (1979) showed no improvements in a range of parenting attitudes (or behaviours) including empathy, acceptance, allowing the child self-direction or involvement with the child, on the part of black parents who had taken part in a brief (four weeks) micro-training parenting programme. There was also evidence to show that participation in a traditional parenting programme (Listening to Children) was not successful in improving attitudes of mostly African-American parents of children with a mean age of five years (Wolfe, 1997). While there was no improvement in trust, acceptance or involvement, there was an improvement in authoritative parenting practices and overall attitudes. The numbers in this study were, however, small.

As with black parents a number of studies showed no significant changes in Hispanic parents' attitudes following participation in a parenting programme. One study showed no significant differences between Hispanic parents who participated in a translated parenting programme (Exploring Parenting) and a control group on five attitudes – creativity, tolerance of frustration, confidence in taking a teaching role, control and play (Copeland, 1981). A number of studies also showed that there were no improvements in parent perceptions about school or education on the part of

Hispanic parents who had taken part in an adapted version of the Systematic Training for Effective Parenting programme (Davis, 1994).

Parent behaviour

A small number of studies measured the impact of a parenting programme on the behaviour of black parents. For example, parents who had taken part in a mother's discussion group interacted more with their children, and were more likely to expand on the children's ongoing play (Slaughter, 1983). They were also more likely at the end of the first but not the second year of the programme to score better than the control mothers on measures of openness and flexibility. This study found that discussion group mothers were significantly superior to controls as regards ego development and maternal teaching style (ibid.).

There was also a significant improvement in levels of verbal and corporal punishment, anger, and stress following participation in a traditional parenting programme on the part of ethnically mixed parents (Nicholson and others, 2002). There was, however, no significant improvement in nurturance, expectations, or stress arising specifically from the parent role.

Mental health

There is evidence to show that parenting programmes can significantly improve the mental health of white parents, including stress, depression and self-esteem (Barlow, Coren and Stewart-Brown, 2002). Similarly, many of the included studies showed an impact on the mental health of minority ethnic parents. A number of studies evaluated the effectiveness of parenting programmes in improving parental stress. For example, participation in the EBPP programme improved parents' stress as regards the overall pressure of parenting, in addition to stresses arising from parent–child interactions (Pitts, 2001). There was also a significant improvement in parent stress relating to the child's capacity for self-regulation following participation in a traditional parenting programme (Listening to Children) (Wolfe, 1997). Two further studies showed that a translated filial therapy programme was effective in significantly improving parent stress in relation to their perceptions of their skills as a parent, and parent stress relating to children's behaviour, moods, and personality (Chau and Landreth, 1997; Yuen, 1997).

There was evidence to show significant improvement in levels of depression in Chinese-American parents enrolled in a Chinese language school in northern California who took part in a culturally specific (SITCAF) parenting programme.

There was evidence of improvement in two aspects of parent locus of control including efficacy and responsibility but not child control, fatalism, or parent control (Ying, 1999).

Some programmes did not, however, improve mental health outcomes. Moore (1992) showed that neither a culturally specific parenting programme (Parents Reclaiming African Information for Spiritual Enlightenment – PRAISE) nor a traditional parenting programme (Preparing for Drug Free Years – PDYF) had any effects on substance use or attitudes towards substance use of African-American parents of adolescent children. A further study showed no improvements in stress for Hispanic parents who had taken part in either a Rational-Emotive Behavioural Therapy (REBT) parenting programme or a standard behavioural parenting programme, compared with the control group (Perez-Nieves, 2001).

Parenting competence

Parenting programmes often aim to impact on the parenting competence of participants, and there was evidence to show improvement in this particular outcome. For example, black parents who took part in the culturally specific EBPP were significantly more likely to feel confident in their role as parents (i.e. able to adequately meet the demands of parenthood and not overly concerned about difficulties in the parent–child relationship), more likely to embrace and encourage the 'reciprocal exchange of emotional and intellectual aspects of living', and more likely to feel that their child's behaviour was caused by a combination of parent–child interaction and environmental influences such as the parents' behaviour and attitude, than by inherited or external factors which are immutable (Pitts, 2001). This programme did not, however, impact on trust, or acceptability (i.e. the extent to which the parent was satisfied with the child and viewed the child as an individual in their own right). Two further studies showed that traditional parenting programmes were effective in improving perceptions of ethnically mixed parents concerning their parenting competence (Mendez-Baldwin, 2001; Percy and McIntyre, 2001).

While one study showed no improvement in the parents' perceived competence or ability to be a parent, or in satisfaction (i.e. parents' frustration, anxiety and motivation) following participation of African-American parents in a culturally specific (Effective Black Parenting) or a culturally adapted (Parent to Parent) programme, these results may be due to the fact that there were significant differences between the two groups at the outset as regards parents' age, employment and income. In addition, the sample size may not have been large enough to ensure that significant differences were detected. A further study also showed no improvements in parent competence for Hispanic parents who had taken part in either a Rational-Emotive Behavioural Therapy (REBT) parenting programme or a standard behavioural parenting programme, compared with the control group (Perez-Nieves, 2001).

Problem solving

Many parenting programmes aim to impact on the problem solving abilities of participating parents. There was evidence from one study to show changes in maternal child-rearing style including the use of problem solving in black inner-city mothers of children with a mean age of four years following participation in an interpersonal cognitive problem solving skills programme (Shure and Spivack, 1978). There was a significant increase in maternal means-end thinking capacity, e.g. capacity to conceptualise step-by-step plans to handle hypothetical problems.

Racial identity

A number of the included studies focused in particular on issues pertaining to racial identity, and there was evidence to show significant improvements in feelings of security concerning racial identity in African-American parents who took part in a culturally specific as opposed to a culturally adapted parenting programme (Schutt-Aine, 1994).

Social support

There was evidence to show that a traditional parenting programme was effective in improving parent attitudes and perceptions concerning family social support on the part of ethnically mixed parents (Mendez-Baldwin, 2001). This study was a one-group design, however, and the results should therefore be treated with caution. A further study showed that there was no improvement in sources of social support or perceived helpfulness of available support in low-income black adolescent single mothers of children aged one to three years following participation in a brief (five weekly sessions) traditional parenting programme (Project APPLY) (Booker, 1986).

Knowledge of childcare/development

Many parenting programmes, particularly those aimed at younger (i.e. adolescent) parents, aim to improve knowledge about childcare and/or development. None of the studies that evaluated this outcome, however, showed any evidence of effectiveness. One study showed that a traditional parenting programme (Project APPLY – Adolescent Parenting Programme – Learning as Youth) did not improve knowledge about child development or environmental influences among 50 low-income black adolescent single mothers of children aged one to three years. The authors suggest that the reasons for this may be that the programme did not include enough sessions (n=5) and that the adolescent low-income participants may well have participated for financial reasons (i.e. a stipend was paid to participating parents). A second study also showed that there were no significant improvements in parent knowledge of child development principles following a culturally adapted version of STEP (Villegas, 1977).

Fostering skills

Two of the included studies evaluated the effectiveness of parenting programmes with foster parents, but only one examined their impact on fostering skills. Carten (1986) compared the effectiveness of a behavioural parenting programme (Independent Life Skills Preparation Project) for black foster parents with a Communication Interaction Programme that was attended by both foster parents and adolescents, in improving the following fostering skills – self awareness, adolescent development, assessment/planning black family life, behaviour management, and system negotiation. Overall, the Communication Interaction group performed slightly better on the above fostering skills compared with the behaviour management group. It should be noted that the numbers in this study were too small to identify significant improvements, and also that improvement in fostering skills was assessed using a non-standardised instrument that was designed for the purpose of the study.

Family outcomes

Family outcomes were assessed in one of the included studies. Moore (1992) showed that participation in a culturally specific parenting programme (Parents Reclaiming African Information for Spiritual Enlightenment – PRAISE) produced significant improvements in family cohesion and expressiveness for a group of African-American parents of adolescent children. This study also showed that there were no improvements in family communication, in particular the extent of open communication, problems or barriers to communication, and the degree to which family members screened their communications with other family members.

Summary

Overall, the included studies demonstrate a range of positive outcomes for both parents and children. The six most reliable studies that evaluated outcomes for black families show a range of positive results. Although the two smaller studies produced negative results, the four larger studies showed effectiveness for traditional, translated and culturally specific programmes. These studies also provide evidence of improvement in both parent and independent assessments of children's emotional and behavioural adjustment, intellectual development, problem solving ability and play, parenting attitudes and behaviour (including the use of harsh and inconsistent discipline), parent stress, and parent–child interaction. However, all studies included outcomes for which there was evidence of no effect. A number of studies in which no evidence of effect were obtained had either methodological problems or problems as regards the delivery/content of the programme.

While the results of the eight studies evaluating outcomes for Hispanic families were not uniformly positive, the findings for the five most reliable studies show evidence of improvement in both parent perceptions and independent assessments of children's emotional and behavioural adjustment. There was also evidence of improvement in parenting attitudes including positive and competent parenting, a reduction in critical parenting, and in parent involvement in education, and bonding with the school and teachers.

Only two studies evaluated the effectiveness of a parenting programme for Native American parents, one of which was a traditional programme and the other was a culturally specific programme. Only one of these two studies included a control group. There was, however, evidence of some improvement in a range of outcomes including parent perceptions concerning children's emotional well-being and behaviour, self-esteem, avoidance of crime and drugs. There was also evidence of effectiveness in improving parent empathy (communication of acceptance, allowing the child self-direction, and involvement), and a range of parenting attitudes and behaviours.

Only four studies evaluated the effectiveness of parenting programmes for groups of ethnically mixed parents. Two of the four studies included a control group, and there was evidence from these studies of some improvement in children's emotional and behavioural adjustment, and learning problems. There was also evidence of some improvement in parenting attitudes and behaviour including levels of verbal and corporal punishment, anger and stress.

Are parenting programmes more effective for parents in some minority ethnic groups than others?

In order to address whether parenting programmes are more effective for parents in some minority ethnic groups than others, a direct comparison of parents from different ethnic groups within one study is necessary. Two studies directly compared outcomes for parents of different minority ethnic groups in this way. The first study was a randomised controlled trial to evaluate the effectiveness of a translated Incredible Years Programme in improving a range of child and parent outcomes in four ethnically diverse groups – African-American, Hispanic, Asian and white (Reid, Webster-Stratton and Beauchaine, 2001). The second study provided a summary of the findings from 143 projects comprising 449 parenting classes and a sample of 3,080 families who had taken part in the culturally specific SMFC programme (Steele and others, 2002). Participating families were from the following ethnic groups – Black, Hispanic, Asian/Pacific Islander, Native Indian and white. This was a one-group study, however, and the results should therefore be treated with caution.

Child outcomes

Both of the comparative studies evaluated the effectiveness of parenting programmes in improving children's emotional and behavioural adjustment. The most rigorous of the two studies (Reid, Webster-Stratton and Beauchaine, 2001) provided parent reports on two measures of child conduct and one measure of social competence: (a) externalising behaviour problems; (b) intensity of problems; and (c) a combined measure of social competence (including positive social behaviours, frustration, tolerance and communication skills) following their participation in the Incredible Years Programme. The white parents reported negligible improvements across all three parent measures of outcome (this result is not reported in section 'Results of quantitative studies' at the end of this chapter). African-American parents reported negligible effects for the two measures of children's behaviour but improvements in social competence. Hispanic parents reported improvements across the two measures of child behaviour but negligible improvement in social competence, and Asian parents reported improvement across all three domains. Independent observations were also obtained on three aspects of child behaviour: (a) positive affect; (b) poor conduct; and (c) a combined measure of deviance, non-compliance and oppositional behaviour. The behaviour of white children showed moderate improvement in conduct and in the combined measure of deviance but negligible improvement in positive affect. African-American children showed small improvements in positive affect and conduct but negligible effects in the combined measure of deviance. Independent observations of Hispanic children showed a small improvement in conduct but negligible improvement in positive affect or the combined measure of child deviance, and Asian children showed improved child deviance and positive affect, but negligible improvement as regards poor conduct.

In the second comparative study, parents who had taken part in the SMFC programme were asked to report on their perceptions concerning their child's ability to feel good about themselves (self-esteem); manage/express feelings or emotions; control behaviour (self-discipline); consider others when making decisions; ask for help/guidance if needed; avoid using or dealing drugs; avoid violence and stay out of gangs; and feel comfortable with his/her ethnicity (Steele and others, 2002). A composite score was calculated for each ethnic group and the results show that there was moderate improvement for Native Indian, Asian, Hispanic and white parents, and a small improvement for African-American parents.

Parent outcomes

The two comparative studies both evaluated the effectiveness of a parenting programme in improving parenting behaviours. The most rigorous study evaluated the effectiveness of the Incredible Years Programme in improving parents' use of harsh or inconsistent discipline and the frequency of their activities with their child (i.e. involvement). The results show that white parents reported moderate improvement in their use of harsh and inconsistent discipline but negligible improvement in their involvement with the child; African-American parents reported a small improvement in involvement but negligible improvement in the use of harsh and inconsistent discipline practices; Hispanic parents reported large improvements across all three domains; and Asian parents reported negligible improvement across all three domains.

Independent observations were also obtained of the parents' use of harsh or critical parenting, competent parenting, positive parenting, and parent commands. White parents showed a small to moderate improvement on all outcomes apart from harsh parenting in which there was negligible change. African-American parents showed moderate to large improvement in all outcomes except parent perceptions concerning their use of commands, which was negligible. Both Asian and Hispanic parents showed small to moderate improvement on all five outcomes.

The Reid, Webster-Stratton and Beauchaine (2001) study also used teacher reports to measure three aspects of the parent's involvement with the school: (a) parent involvement in education; (b) the mother's bond with the school; and (c) the teacher's bond with the parent. The results show that teachers reported large improvements in involvement in education across all four ethnic groups, the smallest improvement being for white parents and the largest improvement for Hispanic parents. They also reported large improvements in the mother's bond with the school for all apart from African-American parents, and improvement in the teacher's bond with the parents for all ethnic groups other than white parents, for which there was only a small change.

The second comparative study provided parents' reports on the following aspects of their parenting ability to manage anger; express emotions; teach child right from wrong; handle child fighting or destructive behaviour; handle child refusal to do housework; make suggestions to child's teacher; make plans to achieve personal goals; access community resources; relationship with children; relationship with other family members (Steele and others, 2002). A composite score was calculated for each ethnic group and the results show moderate change across all ethnic groups.

This study also asked parents to report on the following aspects of their relationship with their child/children: the frequency with which they, kiss or hug their child; yell or holler at the children; have fun together as a family; threaten or criticise the children; talk about the dangers of drugs/gangs; hit or spank the children; spend time with individual children; acknowledge (praise) good behaviour; family discussions to establish rules; go to cultural events together; get angry when child makes mistakes; talk about sexual responsibility; and listen to or ask for their child's opinions or ideas (ibid.). A composite score was once again calculated for each ethnic group and the results show that there was moderate change for Native Indian, Hispanic and Asian parents but only small change for white and African-American parents.

Summary

Overall, the results of these two studies suggest that parenting programmes (both traditional and culturally specific) produced moderate improvements in both positive and negative aspects of parenting in all ethnic groups. The smaller changes in children's behaviour in the Reid, Webster-Stratton and Beauchaine (2001) study are consistent with the results of other prevention studies, the small effects being due to the fact that many children did not have behaviour problems at the outset.

Which parenting programmes are most effective?

The remainder of this chapter examines the relative effectiveness of traditional compared with culturally specific parenting programmes.

Comparative studies

Four studies undertook comparisons of the effectiveness of different types of parenting programme for minority ethnic parents. These studies are important because they provide the only available evidence of the comparative effectiveness of traditional and culturally sensitive parenting programmes. One study compared a culturally specific parenting programme (PRAISE) with a traditional parenting programme (PDYF) (Moore, 1992). One study provided a comparison of a culturally specific parenting programme (EBPP) and a culturally adapted programme (not named) (Schutt-Aine, 1994), and two further studies provided comparisons of adapted parenting programmes. Alvy (1988) compared three adapted parenting programmes (STEP, PET and Confident Parenting), and Carten (1986) compared the effectiveness of two culturally adapted parenting programmes – a behaviour management programme and a communication programme.

Culturally specific versus traditional parenting programmes

Moore (1992) found that both the PDYF and PRAISE intervention groups exhibited greater positive change in parent–child communication, family environment and parent rules/use of alcohol and cigarettes relative to controls. However, only the PRAISE group showed significant improvements in family environment. While this study suggests that parents who attended the PRAISE programme became more committed to their families, more supportive of their children, and had more effective communication with other family members, these improvements may have been due to the higher pre-test scores of the control groups on this variable and the fact that individuals who score very high or very low at one point in time tend to score nearer the average on subsequent measures. It is not therefore clear that this improvement was a result of the intervention. In addition, the small numbers in the PDYF group reduced the likelihood of identifying significant findings in this group.

Culturally specific versus culturally adapted

Schutt-Aine (1994) compared a modified culturally sensitive parenting programme (EBPP) with a culturally adapted programme (Parent to Parent). The results show limited evidence of effectiveness on any of the outcomes measured, and the author of this dissertation suggests that initial differences between the two groups along with small sample size at post-test due to attrition preclude the possibility of reaching any meaningful conclusions.

Comparisons of adapted parenting programmes

One of the included studies compared three parenting programmes – PET, STEP and Confident Parenting. Each of these programmes was adapted to meet the cultural needs of black parents. For example, units were developed and included with specific relevance for black parents such as Pride in Blackness and Black Discipline (Alvy, 1988). The project to adapt these programmes consisted of a number of research and development activities in which: (i) multiracial staff and black mental health, child development and educational experts critiqued the parenting texts of the standard programmes; and (ii) intensive child-rearing interviews were conducted with black and white parents in order to obtain each group's world view or frame of reference concerning child-rearing, and to address specific issues such as how black parents related to issues of blackness in their relationships with their children. These combined data were used to develop a profile of Effective Black Parenting that was then used to modify and adapt the existing parenting programmes.

The adapted programmes were evaluated as part of a pilot study in which both black and white parent training instructors (two who delivered the PET programme, two who delivered the STEP programme and two who delivered a behavioural child management programme called Confident Parenting) were assigned to teach an adapted version of their programme with a group of black Head Start parents. The results show that there was considerable variation in programme attendance and that high attendance was associated with significantly better outcomes. There were significant improvements in acceptance and rejection in parents who took part in the Confident Parenting and PET programmes, but no significant improvement for parents who took part in the STEP programme. There were similarly large changes for all groups as regards parent ratings of relationship change with both preschool and older children (Alvy, 1988).

A further study compared the effectiveness of two culturally adapted parenting programmes – a behaviour management programme and a communication programme – with 20 black foster parents of adolescents (Carten, 1986). While both programmes were implemented on a two-hourly basis over an eight week period, they differed in terms of group composition, i.e. the behaviour management programme was attended only by parents, and the Communication Interaction Programme was attended by both foster parents and adolescents. They also differed in terms of the instructional format used, i.e. the behaviour management programme utilised a didactic teaching format and the Communication Interaction Programme, a process-oriented format focusing on the interactional/communication patterns of the adolescents and foster parents. Both programmes included similar modules.

The results show that there were no significant improvements in fostering skills, in particular as regards self-awareness for parents who took part in the Communication Interaction Programme. Overall, the Communication Interaction group performed slightly better on the above fostering skills compared with the behaviour management group. It should be noted that the numbers in this study were too small to identify significant improvements, and also that improvement in fostering skills was assessed using a non-standardised instrument that was designed for the purpose of the study.

Non-comparative studies

The results of the comparative studies described above are disappointing in that they do not provide sufficiently reliable or rigorous evidence to draw firm conclusions. In the face of these results it is appropriate to consider whether the studies examining individual programmes can collectively tell us anything about their effectiveness. Six studies examined the effectiveness of culturally specific parenting programmes (e.g. EBPP; SMFC), four evaluated the effectiveness of culturally adapted programmes (e.g. adapted STEP), four evaluated the effectiveness of translated programmes (e.g. Incredible Years Programme; STEP; Filial Therapy) and 16 studies evaluated the effectiveness of traditional parenting programmes (e.g. PET; REBT; behavioural; Interpersonal Cognitive Problem Solving; Social Skills Training, etc.).

The majority of studies aimed to evaluate the effectiveness of traditional or translated programmes and collectively these studies provide clear evidence of their effectiveness in improving a range of outcomes for minority ethnic parents.

The six programmes evaluating the effectiveness of culturally specific programmes show mixed results. For example, while four studies showed improvement in most child outcomes measured, two of the studies did not show improvement in any of the child outcomes measured. All studies showed significant improvements, however, in at least half of the parent outcomes measured. Similarly, the four studies that evaluated adapted parenting programmes showed mixed results. Overall, these studies measured only a small number of outcomes. Three out of a total of 11 parent measures were significant, and four out of six child measures were significant.

The reasons for the variability in the findings for the culturally sensitive (specific and adapted) programmes is twofold. First, the methodological quality of these studies was poor. Four out of ten of these studies were conducted as part of Masters or PhD dissertations. Many of them measured a limited number of outcomes and the majority did not have sufficiently large numbers to detect significant results (i.e. were underpowered). Second, nearly half of the studies in this group evaluated a modified version of the EBPP. The modifications to this programme, and in particular, the reduction in the number of sessions by half, may well have played a significant role in reducing its effectiveness.

Results of quantitative studies

The section is divided into the five major ethnic groups that were researched in the included studies, and within each ethnic group the section is divided by study methodology (the most rigorous designs are presented first). The main parent and child outcomes are presented for each study, and the results column provides details concerning whether the results are significant (i.e. $p < 0.05$) or in the absence of a significance level the size of the effect is presented – effect sizes less than 0.3 are small; 0.4 to 0.6 is medium; and an effect size greater than 0.7 is a large result.

BLACK GROUPS		
Study ID	**Measure**	**Significance level (p=) or effect size (d=)**
Randomised controlled trials		
Pembroke (1980) Parent education programme to improve children's self-concept and moral reasoning n=60	**Parent measures** Discipline **Child measures** Justice Authority Self-esteem Realism Identification – mother	 ns ns p=.07 ns ns ns

	Identification – father	ns
	Identification – teacher	ns
	Identification – friends	ns
	Social interest	p=.03
	Minority identification	ns
Pitts (2001)	**Parent measures**	
	Parenting stress	ns
Modified version of	Parenting stress – child	p<.005
Effective Black	Parenting stress – parent	p<.005
Parenting Programme	Parent confidence	p<.005
	Causation	p<.005
n=43	Understanding	p<.005
	Trust	ns
	Acceptability	ns
	Child measures	
	Behaviour	ns
	Externalising behaviour (Teacher report)	ns
Reid and others	**Parent measures**	
(2001)[1]	Harsh discipline	d=.09
	Inconsistent discipline	d=.06
Incredible Years	Frequency of activities with child	d=.19
Parenting Programme	Harsh/critical parenting	d=.41
	Competent parenting	d=.55
n=14 Head Start	Critical parenting	d=.29
centres – 634 parents	Positive parenting	d=.35
	Parent commands	d=.14
	Parent involved in education	d=.59
	Mother bond with school	d=.14
	Teacher bond with parent	d=.68
	Child measures	
	Externalising behaviour	d=.11
	Intensity	d=.06
	Social competence	d=.46
	Child deviance	d=.06
	Child positive affect	d=.29
	Child poor conduct	d=.20
Slaughter (1983)	**Parent measures**	
	Maternal teaching style: interactive (observation)	p<.004
Mothers' Discussion	Maternal teaching style: restrictive	ns
Group	Maternal teaching style: redirective	ns
	Maternal teaching style: directive	ns
n=83	Maternal teaching style: suggestive	ns
	Maternal teaching style: supportive	ns
	Maternal teaching style: expansive	p<.01
	Maternal teaching style: instructive	p<.03
	Maternal teaching style: no theme	ns
	Maternal individuation	ns

	Developmental explanations	ns
	Teaching perspectives	ns
	Ego development	p<.01
	Personal environmental control	ns
	Child measures	
	IQ 41 months	ns
	IQ 32 months	p<.05
	IQ 22 months	p<.05
	Child play structure: inactive (observation)	ns
	Child play structure: transitions	ns
	Child play structure: social contact	ns
	Child play structure: object use non-verbal	p<.01[a]
	Child play structure: object use verbal	p<.02
	Child play structure: grouping non-verbal	ns
	Child play structure: grouping verbal	p<.02
	Child play structure: imitation	ns
	Child play structure: representation	ns

Controlled/comparative studies

Alvy (1988)	**Parent measures**	
	STEP – parent rejection	ns
STEP; PET	PET – parent rejection	p<.01
Confident Parenting	Confident Parenting Programme – parent rejection	p<.05
Programme		
n=48		
Booker (1996)	**Parent measures**	
	Knowledge of infant development	ns
Short-term parent	Knowledge of care	ns
education programme	Number of support sources available	ns
	Perceived degree of helpfulness of support sources	ns
n=57		
Carten (1986)	**Parent measures**	
	Fostering skills	ns
Independent Life Skills	Self-awareness	ns
Preparation Project	Assessment planning/black family life	ns
and Communication	Behaviour management	ns
Interaction Programme	System negotiation	ns
for foster parents		
	Child measures	
n=14	Adolescent development	ns

Creswell-Betsch (1979)	**Parent measures**	
	Empathy: total score	ns
	Communication of acceptance	ns
Micro training and a reading material based programme	Allowing the child self-direction	ns
	Involvement	ns
	Empathy	ns
n=20		
Gordon-Rosen and Rosen (1984)	**Child measures**	
	Absence from school	ns
	Late to school	ns
Standard Adlerian Parent Study Group using STEP materials	Child behaviour	ns
n=42		
Levant and Slobodian (1981)	**Parent measures**	
	Parent acceptance	ns
Levant and Slattery (1982)	Structuring	ns
	Rules	ns
	Limit setting	ns
Systematic skills training programme	Attending	ns
	Empathetic understanding	ns
	Facilitative genuineness	ns
n=15	Respect	ns
	Conflict resolution	ns
	Child measures	
	Emotionally-tension	p<.01
	Child self-esteem	ns
	Asocial index	ns
	Self disclosure	ns
	Placement breakdowns	ns
Moore (1992)	**'PRAISE' programme**	
	Parent measures	
PRAISE and PDYF	Parents' attitude to alcohol use	ns
	Communication	ns
n=45		
	Family measures	
	Family cohesion	p<.05
	Family environment	ns
	Family expressiveness	p<.05
	'PDFY' programme	
	Parent measures	
	Parents' attitude to alcohol use	ns
	Communication	ns
	Family measures	
	Family cohesion	ns
	Family environment	ns

Myers and others (1992) [2] Cohort 1	**Parent measures**	
	Warmth	p<.02
	Undifferentiated rejection	p<.03
	Hostile rejection	p<.06
Effective Black Parenting Programme	Relationship with target child	p<.02
	Child measures	
n=173	Relationship with other family members – boys	p<.03
	Withdrawn child – boys	p<.03
	Hyperactivity – boys	p<.04
	Sexual behaviour problems – girls	p<.03
	Depression – girls	p<.06
Myers and others (1992) [2] Cohort 2	**Parent measures**	
	Hostile rejection	p<.001
	Undifferentiated rejection	p<.01
	Praise	p.<01
Effective Black Parenting Programme	Hitting/spanking	p<.03
	Child measures	
n=a/a	Delinquent behaviours – boys	p<.01
	Delinquent behaviours – girls	p<.01
	Social competence – girls	p<.05
Norwood and others (1997)	**Child measures**	
	Reading	p<.05
	Mathematics	p<.001
Culturally responsive parenting programme		
n=20		
Schutt-Aine (1994)	**'Effective Black Parenting Programme'** **Parent measures**	
Parent to Parent Programme	Parent competence: total score	d=0.03
	Efficacy	d=-.21
	Satisfaction	d=0.13
Effective Black Parenting Programme	Sense of competence	d=0.2
	Pre-encounter stage	d=1.02
	Encounter stage	d=0.21 [b]
n=35	Immersion stage	d=0.01 [b]
	Internalisation	d=0.09
	'Parent to Parent' Programme **Parent measures**	
	Parent competence: total score	d=-0.1
	Efficacy	d=-0.23
	Satisfaction	d=-.39
	Sense of competence	d=0.0
	Pre-encounter stage	d=0.51
	Encounter stage	d=0.73 [b]
	Immersion stage	d=-0.78 [b]
	Internalisation stage	d=0.49

Shure and Spivack (1978)	Parent measures	
	Child-rearing style	p<.001
	Adult problem solving	p<.01
Interpersonal Cognitive Problem Solving Skills programme	**Child measures**	
	Consequential thinking	p<.002
	Cognitive sensitivity	ns
	Preschool interpersonal problem solving test	p<.001
n=40	Means-ended thinking	p<.001
	Child impulsiveness inhibited	p<.05
	Concern for others	ns
	Being liked by peers	ns
	Autonomy	ns
	Initiative	ns
Wolfe (1997)	**Parent measures**	
	Parent stress	p<.03
Listening to Children	Parent stress	p<.09
Programme	Parent stress	p<.004
	Authoritative parenting	p<.006
n=28	Parent attitude: involvement	ns
	Parent attitude: total score	ns

One group design		
Steele and others (2002)	**Parent measures**	
	Parent–child interactions (measured by 13 items)	12 sig at p<.05
	Parent competence (measured by 10 items)	10 sig at p<.001
Strengthening Families Strengthening Communities Programme	**Child measures**	
	Child competence (measured by 8 items)	8 sig at p<.005
n=parents from 143 projects and 449 classes		
Wolfe (1997)	**Parent measures**	
	Difficult child scale	p<.02
Listening to Children	Parent acceptance	ns
Programme	Trust (HPAS)	ns
	Parent attitude: total score	p<.01
n=28	Revaluation counselling ideas scale	p<.01

Retrospective study		
Parker Scott[3] (1999) Parent education programmes for parents of male juveniles n=104	**Child measure** Six month re-arrest	p<.004

1. Results based on additional information provided by the author.
2. Only significant results were presented in the paper.
3. Results based secondary data analysis of data provided in the original dissertation.
a This finding favoured the comparison group
b It is not clear in the paper whether a large effect size for this subscale represents improvement or deterioration

HISPANIC GROUPS		
Study ID	**Measure**	**Significance level (p=) or effect size (d=)**
Randomised controlled trials		
Davis (1994) Modified Systematic Training for Effective Parenting programme n=104	**Parent measures** Parents' perceptions of school and education **Child measures** Mathematics Reading Language Action for disciplinary referrals Child's attitude (Students' Attitude Measure)	ns p=.7 ns p=.003 p=.5 p=.003
Perez-Nieves (2001) Behavioural programme Rational Emotive Therapy programme n=30	**'REBT'** **Parent measures** Parent depression Parent stress Parent stress: competence Parent stress: distractibility **Child measures** Hyperactivity Attention problems **'Behavioural'** **Parent measures** Parent depression	ns ns ns ns ns ns ns

	Parent stress	ns
	Parent stress: competence	ns
	Parent stress: distractibility	ns
	Child measures	
	Hyperactivity	ns
	Attention problems	ns
Reid and others (2001)[1]	**Parent measures**	
	Harsh discipline	d=.61
	Inconsistent discipline	d=.61
Incredible Years Parenting Programme	Frequency of activities with child	d=.65
	Harsh/critical parenting	d=.06
	Competent parenting	d=.26
n=14 Head Start centres – 634 parents	Critical parenting	d=.29
	Positive parenting	d=.59
	Parent commands	d=.17
	Parent involved in education	d=1.19
	Mother bond with school	d=.79
	Teacher bond with parent	d=.98
	Child measures	
	Externalising behaviour	d=.26
	Intensity	d=.35
	Social competence	d=.06
	Child deviance	d–.09
	Child positive affect	d=.06
	Child poor conduct	d=.20
Villegas (1977)	**Parent measures**	
	Knowledge of child development	p=.091
Standard Adlerian parent training programme	**Child measures**	
	Child behaviour	p<.001
n=28		
	Controlled/comparative studies	
Copeland (1981)	**Parent measures**	
Exploring Parenting Curriculum	Parents' attitude: total score	ns
	Parents' attitude: total score	ns
n=80		

Leal (1985) [2] Several different unnamed programmes n=182	**Parent measures** Improved participation in school activities I desire parenting training I personally would like to go back to school I wish there were other parents I could talk with I desire to learn more about parent education I feel that the parenting sessions were very informative I learned new ways to discipline my children I learned how to help my children with their school work I learned how to help my children develop positive self concepts I learned new ways to talk with my children about sex education I enjoy doing things with my children I enjoy being a parent I like making personal sacrifice if it helps my children I'm looking forward to my children growing more independent	$p=.001$ $p=.012$ ns ns ns $p=.001$ $p=.001$ $p=.001$ $p=.001$ $p=.001$ ns ns ns ns

One group design

Steele and others (2002) Strengthening Families Strengthening Communities Programme n=parents from 143 projects and 449 classes	**Parent measures** Parent–child interactions (measured by 13 items) Parent competence (measured by 10 items) **Child measures** Child competence (measured by 8 items)	13 sig at $p<.05$ 10 sig at $p<.001$ 8 sig at $p<.001$

Retrospective study

Parker Scott (1999)[3] Parent education programmes for parents of male juveniles n=210	**Child measure** Six month re-arrest	ns

1. Results based on additional information provided by the author.
2. Many outcomes that were measured were not reported.
3. Only significant results were presented in the paper.

ASIAN (CHINESE AMERICAN /ASIAN PACIFIC ISLANDERS) GROUPS		
Study ID	Measure	Significance level (p=) or effect size (d=)
Randomised controlled trials		
Chau and Landreth (1997) **Chau (1996)** Filial Therapy parenting programme n=36	**Parent measures** Empathy: total score Communication of acceptance Allowing the child self-direction Involvement Parent stress Parent stress Parent stress Parent acceptance: total score Respect for child Appreciation of child Recognition of child's need for autonomy Unconditional love	p<.001 p<.001 p<.001 p<.001 p<.001 p<.001 p<.001 p<.001 p<.001 p<.001 p<.001 p<.001
Reid and others (2001)[1] Incredible Years Parenting Programme n=14 Head Start centres – 634 parents	**Parent measures** Harsh discipline Inconsistent discipline Frequency of activities with child Harsh/critical parenting Competent parenting Critical parenting Positive parenting Parent commands Parent involved in education Mother bond with school Teacher bond with parent Externalising behaviour Intensity **Child measures** Social competence Child deviance Child positive affect Child poor conduct	d=.06 d=.06 no effect d=.40 d=.29 d=.59 d=.55 d=.25 d=.58 d=.59 d=.66 d=.31 d=.71 d=.41 d=.52 d=.25 d=.14
Yuen (1997) Filial Therapy parenting programme n=35	**Parent measures** Empathy: total score Communication of acceptance Allowing child self direction Involvement Parent acceptance: total score Respect for child Appreciation of child Recognition of child's need for autonomy	p=.015 p<.001 p<.001 p<.003 p<.001 p<.001 p<.001 p<.001

	Unconditional love	p<.001
	Parent stress	p<.001
	Parent stress	p<.001
	Parent stress	p<.001
	Problem behaviour	p<.001
	Child measures	
	Self perception	ns
	Child competence	p<.001
One group designs		
Steele and others (2002) Strengthening Families Strengthening Communities Programme n= parents from 143 projects and 449 classes	**Parent measures** Parent child interactions (measured by 13 items) Parent competence (measured by 10 items) **Child measures** Child competence (measured by 8 items)	 11 sig at p<.001 10 sig at p<.001 8 sig at p<.001
Ying (1999) Programme designed to reduce intergenerational conflict in migrant families n=30	**Parent measures** Parent efficacy Parent responsibility Child's control Fatalism/chance Parent control Intergenerational relationships Depression Parent's sense of coherence Social desirability **Child measures** Child's self-esteem	 p<.05 p<.01 ns ns ns p<0.05 ns ns ns ns

1. Results-based secondary data analysis of data provided in the original dissertation.

NATIVE AMERICAN GROUPS		
Study ID	Measure	Significance level (p=) or effect size (d=)
Controlled/comparative study		
Glover and Landreth (2000) Filial Therapy parenting programme n=25	**Parent measures** Parent stress Parent stress Parent stress Empathy: total score Communication of acceptance Allowing child self direction Involvement Parent acceptance: total score Respect for child Appreciation of child Recognition of child's need for autonomy Unconditional love **Child measures** Child behaviour: total score Child behaviour: sustained play Child behaviour: self-directiveness Child behaviour: parent/child connectedness Child self-esteem	ns ns ns p<.001 p<.001 p<.001 p<.001 ns ns ns ns ns p=.003 ns p=.001 p=.002 ns
One group design		
Steele and others (2002) Strengthening Families Strengthening Communities Programme n=parents from 143 projects and 449 classes	**Parent measures** Parent–child interactions (measured by 13 items) Parent competence (measured by 10 items) **Child measures** Child competence (measured by 8 items)	11 sig at p<.05 10 sig at p<.001 8 sig at p<.005

GROUPS OF ETHNICALLY MIXED		
Study ID	Measure	Significance level (p=) or effect size (d=)
Randomised controlled trial		
Nicholson and others (2002)	**Parent measures**	
	Parent behaviour: nurturing	ns
	Parent behaviour: discipline	p<.05
STAR – a	Parent behaviour: expectations	ns
psychoeducational	Parent behaviour: distress	ns
parenting programme	Parent stress: parent	ns
	Parent stress: child	ns
n=26	Parent stress: interaction	p<.05
	Anger-aggression	p<.05
	Parent behaviour – positive	ns
	Parent behaviour – negative	ns
	Child measures	
	Behaviour	p<.05
	Behaviour: problems	ns
	Behaviour: intensity	ns
	Behaviour: problems (teacher report)	ns
	Behaviour: intensity (teacher report)	ns
	Behaviour (parent report)	p<.05
	Behaviour (teacher report)	ns
	Behaviour – positive (observational report)	ns
	Behaviour – negative (observational report)	ns
Controlled/comparative study		
Tulloch (1996)	**Parent measures**	
	Parent's attitude: confidence	ns
SOS behavioural	Parent's attitude: causation	ns
parent training	Parent's attitude: acceptance	ns
programme	Parent's attitude: understanding	ns
	Parent's attitude: trust	ns
n=27		
	Child measures	
	Conduct problems	ns
	Impulse hyperactivity	ns
	Learning problems	ns
	Psychosomatic symptoms	ns
	Anxiety	ns
	Hyperactivity index	ns
	Child behaviour	ns

One group design		
Mendez-Baldwin (2001)	**Parent measures**	
	Parent attitudes	p<.05
	Parenting sense of competence	p<.05
Parent education workshop	**Parent measures**	
	Knowledge about child care	p<.05
n=22	Parenting sense of competence – valuing comfort	ns
Percy and McIntyre (2001)	Parenting competence – total score	p<.05
Programme to improve parent self-confidence		
n=20		

Summary

Overall, the results of the comparative studies are disappointing. They do not provide sufficiently reliable or rigorous evidence to reach any firm conclusions regarding the comparative effectiveness of different parenting programmes, and point to the need for such a study to be conducted. The non-comparative studies provide evidence of the effectiveness of traditional and translated programmes, and more limited evidence of the effectiveness of culturally sensitive programmes. The latter result is largely due to the paucity of high quality research on interventions of this nature.

6. Conclusions

Introduction

The studies included in this review describe the many ways in which parenting programmes can help parents. The data from the small number of qualitative studies confirm the findings of the more numerous quantitative studies and provide a broader insight into the ways in which parents find such programmes helpful. The majority of studies on which the findings of this review are based, however, were conducted in the USA. The experiences of Caribbean parents within the UK is very different to that of African-Americans as a result of the difference in size of the two communities and other factors such as the different welfare state systems in the two countries, which can have an impact on the way in which families are organised. In addition, there were no studies of large UK minority ethnic groups such as parents from Indian or Pakistani communities, and one of the minority ethnic groups included in this review (Hispanic parents) is not numerous in the UK. Thus, while the findings of this review are largely positive, they are not automatically transferable to a UK context. This reflects the fact that while the content of many US programmes are similar to those being used in the UK, the context of such provision is different (e.g. many parents in the US are given payments for taking part in such programmes), as are the life experiences of participating parents. This points to the need to establish a body of evidence concerning the effectiveness of parenting programmes for minority ethnic parents living in the UK.

Are parenting programmes effective for minority ethnic parents?

The majority of studies included in this review evaluated the effectiveness of traditional parenting programmes such as Rational-Emotive Behaviour Therapy,

Filial Therapy, and a range of standard behavioural programmes including the Webster-Stratton Incredible Years Programme. This group of studies comprises the most robust evaluations of the effectiveness of parenting programmes and they provide clear evidence of the effectiveness of traditional programmes in improving a range of important outcomes for parents and children across a diverse range of minority ethnic groups.

With regard to culturally specific programmes the results were more mixed. For example, three studies (one of which comprised two cohorts) evaluated the Effective Black Parenting Programme. In one study, while one cohort of parents showed improvements in parent perceptions of children's emotional and behavioural adjustment (but no improvement in teacher ratings of externalising behaviour), a second cohort showed improvement in social competence and delinquent behaviours (Myers and others, 1992). Similarly, as regards parent attitudes and behaviour, while one study showed no evidence of improvement in parents' sense of competence, efficacy and satisfaction (Schutt-Aine, 1984), the most robust study (Pitts, 2001) showed significant improvement in parent stress, a reduction in the use of directive responses compared with non-directive, and improvement in a number of parent attitudes including confidence. The variability in these findings is possibly due to methodological issues and modifications that were made to the programme, and the lack of strong evidence supporting culturally sensitive parenting programmes is therefore a reflection of this.

The results from the four studies evaluating the effectiveness of culturally adapted versions of parenting programmes (e.g. STEP, PET, and Confident Parenting) include only a small number of outcomes (i.e. only one assessed parent perceptions of children's behaviour), and the findings are, once again, mixed. One study, for example, showed the most improvement for parents who attended more regularly (Alvy, 1988). While some of these studies evaluated what are described as 'adapted' versions of the above programmes, in one study (Davis, 1994) it is not clear in what way the programme was adapted to meet the needs of the Hispanic population to whom it was delivered other than the translation of videos, etc., into Spanish.

The existence of more copious and rigorous evaluation of traditional behavioural parenting programmes parallels the situation with regard to the evaluation of parenting programmes with white parents. One of the reasons for this may be that irrespective of the ethnicity of participating parents, it is considerably easier to evaluate the effectiveness of standard behavioural programmes compared with the diverse 'relationship' and culturally specific parenting programmes, which are more wide-ranging in their aims and strategies, and aim to impact on a more diverse set of outcomes.

Only two of the studies included in this review directly compared traditional and culturally specific parenting programmes (Moore, 1992; Schutt-Aine, 1984), and the results do not provide us with sufficiently rigorous evidence to assess their relative effectiveness for minority ethnic parents.

Only two studies directly compared outcomes for parents from different ethnic groups. While the evidence from one of the studies is less reliable than the first due to the fact that no control group was used, both studies provide evidence of the effectiveness of parenting programmes in improving a range of parent and child outcomes for families from all ethnic groups. There was no evidence to indicate greater effectiveness for any one particular ethnic group (white parents included), and the results show improvement across all types of outcomes, i.e. parent and independent observations, child and parent measures.

Some, but not all of the included studies, showed the effectiveness of parenting programmes in improving children's behaviour. This is an important outcome for both parents and society. However, while policy makers may view parenting programmes as a means of promoting social inclusion (Henricson, 2003), the results of the qualitative studies suggest that minority ethnic parents perceived the benefits of these programmes in wider terms. Perhaps most importantly they talked about improved relationships with their children, and greater enjoyment of being a parent.

Is there a need for culturally specific parenting programmes?

It has been suggested that 'cultural sensitivity' can be demonstrated if programme facilitators help parents to identify 'their own individual goals for their children, and by respecting diverse viewpoints and goals ...' (Reid, Webster-Stratton and Beauchaine, 2001, p.210). This suggests that generic parenting programmes that are directed at diverse ethnic populations can 'be individualised to fit with the specific experiences and backgrounds of group members, without the need for different curricula for participants from different backgrounds' (ibid.). In support of this stance, a number of studies have shown that both generic and culturally focused drug and alcohol prevention programmes for example, appear to be equally effective in producing positive change in both minority ethnic and white populations (Botvin and others, 1994; 1995 in Reid, Webster-Stratton and Beauchaine, 2001). It has also been argued that given the cost of developing, evaluating, and implementing culturally specific programmes and the increasing heterogeneity of the parent population, the use of generic programmes, if effective, is desirable (Reid, Webster-Stratton and Beauchaine, 2001).

These are powerful arguments. However, recent research by the Race Equality Unit (REU) (Butt and Box, 1998) showed that some minority ethnic families felt that parenting education 'was not for them' primarily because of the way in which parenting techniques and strategies were presented in traditional parenting programmes. There is, in addition, a high drop out of minority ethnic parents from traditional parenting programmes (Holden, Lavigne and Cameron, 1990; Strain, Young and Horowitz, 1981). While the drop out rate for minority ethnic parents may not be any higher than that for some other groups (i.e. the average drop out rate for parents in some parenting programmes is in the region of 30 per cent and can be as high as 50 per cent), any drop out, irrespective of ethnic group, may reflect the fact that the parenting programme has failed to meet the needs of the parents who finished prematurely. In the case of minority ethnic parents it may well reflect the mismatch between the values of the programme providers and those of the participating parents.

The use of culturally specific parenting programmes is based on two arguments. First, that the needs of minority ethnic parents are not being met by traditional parenting programmes. This refers in particular to the fact that minority ethnic parents have needs that are distinct from parents who are members of the dominant culture. This position was supported in Chapter 1 where it was argued that minority ethnic parents have a number of additional parenting tasks when they are located within a culture that is different from their own. Parenting programmes that fail to recognise these additional tasks are as such failing to meet the specific needs of minority ethnic parents, based on the ethnocentric assumption that all parents' needs are the same irrespective of race and culture. There is, in addition, a more specific concern that traditional parenting programmes are based on values that are fundamentally different from the values of the participating parents. That this is in fact the case was very powerfully demonstrated by the data obtained from Chinese-American parents who had taken part in a traditional filial therapy parenting programme. Filial Therapy Parenting Programmes are based on 'child centred' approaches to child-rearing, which emphasise the importance of child autonomy and freedom, and the creation of an environment in which children feel safe to express their thoughts and feelings. Such values are diametrically opposed to those that have been described as being characteristic of Chinese culture such as, for example, obedience to authority, and the expression only of emotions that are 'harmonious'. While some mental health professionals in China are beginning to question whether these values are helpful for the socialisation of children (Chau and Landreth, 1997), the fact remains that Chinese-American parents have a very different value system to those of American and European parents, and to the values underpinning many traditional parenting programmes (including translated parenting programmes).

The qualitative data in this review suggested that parents could benefit from parenting programmes even where the parents' core cultural values were being challenged. Most of the data supporting this argument was obtained from Chinese-American parents who had taken part in a traditional parenting programme. As was argued in an earlier chapter, Chinese-American parents may be unrepresentative of other minority ethnic parents, in part due to the emphasis of Chinese culture on obedience. Although culturally specific parenting programmes may also challenge the parenting practices of particular groups of parents, this is done with particular care as regards the cultural sensitivities of parents. The Effective Black Parenting Programme (EBPP), for example, challenges what are suggested to be traditional black values concerning the discipline of children through the location of such values and practices within the historical trajectory of black people. Similarly, the use of alternative methods of discipline is advocated through an exploration of the current position of black people in society and the civil rights movement. Culturally specific parenting programmes do not thereby risk undermining the culture and values of minority ethnic groups, and to the extent that traditional parenting practices are challenged, such challenges are undertaken in a way that is both respectful of the parents' culture and that takes account of the historical and cultural reasons for the development of particular parenting practices. Also, many culturally specific parenting programmes are developed by or in consultation with members of the minority ethnic group at whom the programme is directed (see for example, Myers and others, 1992 and Norwood and others, 1997). As such, any challenges to traditional parenting practices that are part of the curricula of culturally specific parenting programmes are being made from within a particular minority ethnic group, rather than by members of the dominant culture.

The findings of this review also indicate that culturally specific parenting programmes have 'added value' in terms of their capacity to enhance and support the parents' own cultural values, and to address specific historical traumas that have shaped the parenting practices and the 'ways of living' of different minority ethnic groups. This was exemplified by the case of Native American parents from the Lakota Reservation (Brave Heart, 1999). These parents indicated that taking part in a culturally specific parenting programme had made them more aware of important aspects of their culture that had been lost to them, and also more aware of the role that displacement to boarding schools had played in the lives of their forefathers. Such knowledge had enabled them to move on from the trauma that had played such a significant role in the lives of their parents and grandparents, and which had continued to shape their own parenting practices. Such knowledge had also enabled them to re-establish links with family members with whom they had lost contact.

Future directions

Policy and practice

There is increasing diversity in the parenting population in the UK, and minority ethnic parents represent a significant part of this diversity. It is therefore important that providers of parenting programmes in this country address the specific needs of parents from different ethnic groups.

There are currently very few culturally sensitive parenting programmes available in the UK, and many providers of traditional parenting programmes will be familiar with a situation in which there are one or two minority ethnic parents taking part in a predominantly white group of parents. The results of this review suggest that good practice might include the following:

1. Sensitivity to the fact that parents from minority ethnic groups may endorse different parenting practices as a result of their race and culture. This should not be assumed, however, and programme facilitators might want to spend some time exploring whether this is the case.

2. Programme facilitators exploring the values underpinning the programme they are providing, and making these explicit, e.g. whether the programme makes assumptions about gender roles, child-rearing attitudes and practices, or about issues relating more specifically to ethnicity and culture.

3. Programme developers incorporating multicultural family factors including recognition of diversity in family composition, and the parenting role of others in addition to the child's birth parents.

4. Programme developers and providers acknowledging and supporting diversity in child-rearing attitudes and practices.

5. Programme facilitators making adaptations to their programmes in order to be able to offer courses that are specifically directed at meeting the needs of parents from different minority ethnic groups.

6. Programme facilitators providing extra support to minority ethnic parents whose value system and parenting practices are being challenged by the values of the parenting programme.

7. Programme facilitators making themselves aware of other programmes that are available locally, especially culturally specific programmes, which may be better placed to address the specific needs of a parent from a particular minority ethnic group.

Although the evidence base to support the effectiveness of culturally specific parenting programmes is not strong, this is the result of inadequate research rather than clear evidence of ineffectiveness. The qualitative studies strongly suggest that these programmes can have 'added value' for parents from different minority ethnic groups. However, parenting programmes are still a relatively new phenomenon, and there is considerable variation in their local availability, and a paucity nationally of programmes that have been designed specifically to take account of the needs of parents from different ethnic groups. One result of this situation is that most parents are forced to avail themselves of whatever programme is on offer locally, the choice of which very often reflects the preoccupations and predilections of the professionals providing the programme in both the voluntary and statutory sectors. The use of particular programmes is also being driven by available evidence, and as was suggested earlier, there is currently considerably more evidence available to support the use of behavioural as opposed to the more diverse 'relationship' based and culturally specific parenting programmes.

Greater availability of parenting programmes and greater commitment of programme developers and providers to making explicit the values underpinning parenting programmes will enable parents to make more informed choices about the type of programme that they attend. In particular, it may enable parents from minority ethnic groups to avail themselves of parenting support that pays particular attention to the concerns and issues faced by parents who are not part of the dominant culture.

Research

The absence of any UK-based studies, and the paucity of rigorous research more generally, point to the need for further evaluation of the effectiveness of culturally specific parenting programmes in the UK, and in particular for comparison of the relative effectiveness of traditional parenting programmes such as the Webster-Stratton Incredible Years Programme with culturally specific programmes such as the Strengthening Parents Strengthening Communities programme. Such an evaluation would need to pay careful consideration to the different foci of the two programmes in terms of the fact that they may be aimed at improving different types of outcomes. For example, the Incredible Years Programme might place more emphasis on children's behaviour, while the Strengthening Parents programme might emphasise enhancing children's racial identity. This points to the need for careful thought in terms of the types of outcomes being measured, and the way in which the findings of such a study are reported. It seems likely that a study of this nature might show that different programmes help parents to do different things, and that one is not therefore better or superior to another. This would support the need to give parents choice about the programme in which they participate, in order that they could select a programme that met their particular concerns at any one point in time.

Research is also needed of the experiences of parents who drop out of parenting programmes. We now recognise that minority ethnic parents are more likely to drop out of parenting programmes than white parents. Research from the REU has in addition pointed to some of the concerns of minority ethnic parents about parenting programmes (Butt and Box, 1998). Further work is now needed with parents who have attended one or two sessions of a parenting programme prior to dropping out. It would be particularly interesting to compare the experiences of minority ethnic parents who drop out of a traditional parenting programme with those who drop out of a culturally specific parenting programme.

References

Akinyela, M M (1996) *Black families, cultural democracy and self-determination: An African-centered pedagogy* [dissertation]. Atlanta, GA: Emory University

Alvy, K T (1987) *Parent training: A social necessity.* Studio City, CA: Center for the Improvement of Child Caring

Alvy, K T (1988) 'Parenting programs for black parents' *in* Bond, L A and Wagner, B M *eds Families in Transition*. California: Sage Publications

Auerbach, A (1968) *Parents learn through discussion: principles and practice of parent group education.* New York: Wiley

Auerbach, A (1971) *Creating a preschool center: parent development in an intergrated neighborhood project.* New York: Wiley

Badger, E (1968) *Mothers' training program in educational intervention by mothers of disadvantaged infants.* Washington, D.C.: National Institute of Education

Badger, E (1971) 'A mothers' training program – the road to a purposeful existence', *Children,* 18, 168–73

Badger, E (1973) *Mother's guide to early learning.* Paoli, PA.: McGraw-Hill

Barlow, J and Stewart-Brown, S L (2000) Review article: 'Behavior Problems and Parent-Training Programs', *Journal of Developmental and Behavioral Pediatrics,* 21, 356–70

Barlow, J and Stewart-Brown, S (2001) 'Understanding parenting programmes: parents' views', *Primary Health Care Research and Development,* 2, 117–30

Barlow, J, Coren, E and Stewart-Brown, S (2002) 'Meta-analysis of parenting programmes in improving maternal psychosocial health', *British Journal of General Practice*, 52, 223–33.

Barnes, G M (1984) 'Adolescent alcohol abuse and other problem behaviour: their relationship and common parent influences', *Journal of Youth and Adolescence*, 13, 329–84

Baumrind, D (1985) 'Familial antecedents of adolescent drug use: a developmental perspective' *in* Jones, C L and Battjes, R L eds *Etiology of drug abuse: Implications for preventions* (pp.13–44). NIDA Research Monograph 56, A RAUS Review Report

Baumrind, D (1989) 'Rearing competent children' *in* Damon, W *ed. Child development today and tomorrow* (pp.349–78). San Francisco: Jossey-Bass

Belsky, J and Vondra, J (1989) 'Lessons from child abuse: determinants of parenting' *in* Cicchetti, D and Carlson, V eds *Child Maltreatment: Theory and research on the causes and consequences of child abuse and neglect.* Cambridge University Press

Berman, S F and Rickel, A U (1979) 'Assertive training for low-income black parents', *Clinical Social Work Journal,* 7, 123–32

Booker, B M (1986) *The effects of a short-term parent education program on knowledge of child development, knowledge of environmental influences and varied support variables among low-income black adolescent single mothers* [dissertation]. Georgia State University

Botvin, G J, Schinke, S P, Epstein, J A and Diaz, T (1994) 'Effectiveness of culturally focused and generic skills training approaches to alcohol and drug abuse and minority youths', *Psychology of Addictive Behaviors,* 8, 116–27

Botvin, G J, Schinke, S P, Epstein, J A, Diaz, T and Botvin, E M (1995) 'Effectiveness of culturally focused and generic skills training approaches to alcohol and drug abuse prevention among minority adolescents: two-year follow-up results', *Psychology of Addictive Behaviors,* 9, 183–94

Brave Heart, M Y H (1999) 'Oyate Ptayela: rebuilding the Lakota Nation through addressing historical trauma among Lakota parents', *Journal of Human Behavior in the Social Environment,* 2, 109–26

Brody, G and Flor, D L (1998) 'Maternal resources, parenting practices, and child competence in rural, single-parent African American families', *Child Development,* 69, 803–16

Brown, J, Cohen, P, Johnson, J G and Salzinger, S (1998) 'A longitudinal analysis of risk factors for child maltreatment: findings of a 17-year prospective study of officially recorded and self-reported child abuse and neglect', *Child Abuse and Neglect,* 22, 1065–78

Butt, J and Box, L (1998) *Family Centred: Study of the Use of Family Centres by Black Families.* Race Equality Unit

Carlson, V J. and Harwood, R L (2003) 'Attachment, culture and caregiving system: the cultural patterning of everyday experience among Anglo and Puerto Rican mother-infant', *Infant Mental Health Journal,* 24, 53–73

Carten, A J (1986) *The independent life skills preparation project: A model for the development of a specialized foster parent training program* [dissertation]. City University of New York

Cedar, B and Levant, R F (1990) 'A meta-analysis of the effects of parent-effectiveness training', *American Journal of Family Therapy,* 19, 373–84

Champion, L A, Goodall, G and Rutter, M (1995) 'Behavior problems in childhood and stressors in early adult life: 1. A 20 year follow-up of London school children', *Psychological Medicine,* 25, 231–46

Chau, I Y F (1996) *Filial therapy with Chinese parents* [dissertation]. University of North Texas

Chau, I Y F and Landreth, G L (1997) 'Filial therapy with Chinese parents: effects on parent empathic interactions, parent acceptance of child and parent stress', *International Journal of Play Therapy,* 6, 75–92

Cheng Gorman, J (1996) *Culturally-sensitive parent education programs for ethnic minorities* (PC Reports 7-96-26). New York University, Psychoeducational Center

Cheng Gorman, J and Balter, L (1997) 'Culturally specific Parent Education: A Critical Review of Quantitative Research', *Review of Educational Research,* 67, 339–69

Children's Defense Fund (1985*) Black and White children in America: Key facts.* Washington, D.C.

Clark, R M (1983) *Family life and school achievement: Why poor black children succeed and fail.* Chicago, IL: University of Chicago Press

Cohen, D, Richardson, J and Labree, L (1994) 'Parenting behaviours and the onset of smoking and alcohol use: a longitudinal study', *Pediatrics,* 20, 368–75

Copeland, M L (1981) *The Impact of Participation in Head Start's Exploring Parenting program on Low SES mothers' parent attitudes* [dissertation]. Temple University, Philadelphia

Cox, C B (2002) 'Empowering African American custodial grandparents', *Social Work,* 47, 45–54

Creswell-Betsch, C (1979) *Comparison Of A Family Microtraining Program And A Reading Program To Enhance Empathic Communication By Black Parents With Young Children* [dissertation]. University of Massachusetts

Davis, L A J (1994) *The effect of parent involvement training on the achievement of Hispanic students* [dissertation]. University of North Texas

Day, H R (1995) 'Research and development of Moderated Interactive Training Sessions (MITS): a substance use prevention package for African-American parents of adolescents', *Drugs: Education, Prevention and Policy,* 2, 147–59

Denham, S A, Workman, E, Cole, P M, Weissbrod, C, Kendziora, K T and Zahn-Waxler, C (2000) 'Prediction of externalizing behavior problems from early to middle childhood: the role of parent socialization and emotion expression', *Development and Psychopathology,* 12, 23–45

Department of Health (1995) *Improving the Health of Mothers and Children: NHS Priorities for Research and Development. Report to the NHS Central Research and Development Committee.* NHS

Department of Health (1998) *Modernising Social Services: Promoting Independence, Improving Protection, Raising Standards.* The Stationery Office

Department of Health (1999) *Saving Lives: Our healthier nation.* The Stationery Office

Department of Health (2000) *Excellence Not Excuses: Inspection of Services for Ethnic Minority Children and Families.* Social Services Inspectorate

Eimers, R and Aitchison, R (1977) *Effective parents–responsible child: A guide to confident parenting.* New York: McGraw-Hill

Eisenberg, N (1998) 'Parent socialization of emotion', *Psychological Inquiry,* 9, 241–73

Eisenberg, N, Fabes, R A, Shepard, S A, Guthrie, I K, Murphy, B C and Reiser, M (1999) 'Parent reactions to children's negative emotions: longitudinal relations to quality of children's social functioning', *Child Development,* 70, 513–34

Farrington, D P (1991) 'Childhood aggression and adult violence: early precursors and later life outcomes' *in* Peper, D J and Rubin, K H eds *The development and treatment of childhood aggression* (pp.5–29). Hillsdale, NJ: Lawrence Erlbaum

Gibbs, J T (1984) 'Black adolescents and youth: an endangered species', *American Journal of Orthopsychiatry,* 51, 6–21

Glover, G J and Landreth, G L (2000) 'Filial therapy with Native Americans on the Flathead Reservation', *International Journal of Play Therapy,* 9, 57–80

Gordon-Rosen, M C (1982) *The effects of parent training in the principles and applications of Adlerian psychology on home behavior, school attendance and school achievement of inner-city junior high school students.* George Washington University

Gordon-Rosen, M C and Rosen, A (1984) 'Adlerian Parent Study Groups and inner-city children', *Individual Psychology: Journal of Adlerian Theory, Research and Practice,* 40, 309–16

Grimshaw, R and McGuire, C (1998) *Evaluating Parenting Programmes: A study of stakeholders' views.* National Children's Bureau and Joseph Rowntree Foundation

Gross, D (1996) 'What is a "Good" Parent?', *American Journal of Maternal Child Nursing,* 21, 172–82

Halpern, R (1990) 'Poverty and early childhood parenting: toward a framework for intervention', *American Journal of Orthopsychiatry,* 60, 6–18

Harrison-Ross, P and Kempe, H (1976) *The black child: A parent's guide.* New York: Peter H. Wyden

Hart, B and Ridely, T R (1995) *Meaningful difference in children's everyday lives.* Baltimore, MD: P.H. Brookes Publishing Co.

Henricson, D (2003) *Government and Parenting: Is there a case for a policy review and a parents' code?* Joseph Rowntree Foundation

Holden, G W, Lavigne, V V and Cameron, A M (1990) 'Probing the Continuum of Effectiveness in Parent Training: Characteristics of Parents and Preschoolers', *Journal of Clinical Child Psychology,* 19, 2–8

Holler, B and Hurrelmann, K (1990) 'The role of parent and peer contacts for adolescents' state of health' *in* Hurrelmann, K and Loesel, F eds *Health hazards in adolescence. Prevention and intervention in childhood and adolescence,* 8, 409–32

Hunsley, M and Thoman, E B (2002) 'The sleep of co-sleeping infants when they are not co-sleeping: evidence that co-sleeping is stressful', *Developmental Psychobiology,* 40, 14–22

Hylton, C (1997) *Family Survival Strategies; Moyenda Black Families Talking, An exploring parenthood project*. Joseph Rowntree Foundation

Johnson, R C, Brown, C V, Harris, A and Lewis, E (1980) *Manual of Black Parenting Education*. St Louis, MO: Institute of Black Studies

Kellam, S G, Brown, H C, Rubin, B R and Ensminger, M E (1983) 'Paths leading to teenage psychiatric symptoms and substance use: developmental epidemiological studies in Woodlawn' *in* Guse, S B, Earls, F J and Barrett, J E *eds Childhood Psychopathology and Development* (pp.7–51). New York: Raven Press

Kelley, M L, Sanchez-Hucles, J and Walker, R R (1993) 'Correlates of disciplinary practices in working-to-middle class African-American mothers', *Merrill-Palmer Quarterly*, 39, 252–64

Lau, S, Lew, W J, Hau, K T, Cheung, P C and Berndt, T J (1990) 'Relations among perceived parent control, warmth, indulgence, and family harmony of Chinese in Mainland China', *Developmental Psychology*, 26, 674–7

Leal, O (1985) *An Evaluation Of The Effects Of Parent Training Programs On Attitudes, Skills And Practices* [dissertation]. The University Of Texas At Austin

Levant, R F and Slattery, S C (1982) 'Systematic skills training for foster parents', *Journal of Clinical Child Psychology*, 11, 138–43

Levant, R F and Slobodian, P E (1981) 'The Effects of a Systematic Skills Training Program for Foster Mothers', *Journal of Education*, 163, 262–75

Levine, R (1977) 'Child rearing as cultural adaptation' *in* Leiderman, P H and others eds *Culture and Infancy: variations in Human Experience* (pp.15–27). New York: Academic Press

Lin, C Y and Fu, V R (1990) 'A Comparison of child-rearing practices among Chinese, immigrant Chinese, and White-American parents', *Child Development*, 61, 439–43

Loeber, R and Dishion, T J (1983) 'Early predictors of male delinquency: a review', *Psychological Bulletin*, 94, 68–99

Lundberg, O (1993) 'The impact of childhood living conditions on illness and mortality in adulthood', *Social Science and Medicine*, 36, 1047–52

Lundberg, O (1997) 'Childhood conditions, sense of coherence, social class and adult ill health: exploring their theoretical and empirical relations', *Social Science and Medicine*, 44, 821–31

McClun, L A and Merrell, K W (1998) 'Relationship of perceived parenting styles, locus of control orientation, and self-concept among junior-school age students', *Psychology in the Schools*, 35, 381–90

McCord, J, McCord, W and Howard, A (1963) 'Family interaction as antecedent to the direction of male aggressiveness', *Journal of Abnormal and Social Psychology,* 66, 2239–42

McKenna, J, Mosko, S, Richard, C, Drummond, S and others (1995) 'Experimental studies of infant parent co-sleeping: mutual physiology and behavioural influences and their relevance to SIDS (Sudden infant death syndrome)', *Early Human Development,* 38, 187–201, 381–90

Mendez-Baldwin, M M (2001) *Changes in parent sense of competence and attitudes in low-income Head Start parents as a result of participation in a parent education workshop* [dissertation]. Fordham University, New York

Moffit, T E, Caspi, A, Dickson, N, Silva, P and others (1996) 'Childhood-onset versus adolescent-onset antisocial conduct problems in males: natural history from ages 3 to 18 years', *Developmental Psychology*, 8, 399–424

Moore, V M (1992) *Parent training: Drug abuse inoculation in the nineties* [dissertation]. Georgia State University

Morelli, G A, Rogoff, B, Oppenheim, D and Goldsmith, D (1992) 'Cultural Variation in Infants' Sleeping Arrangements: Questions of Independence', *Developmental Psychology*, 28, 604–12

Myers, H F (1989) 'Urban stress and mental health in Afro-American youth: an epidemiological and conceptual update' *in* Jones, R *ed. Black Adolescents*. Berkley, CA: Cobb and Henry

Myers, H F, Alvy, K T, Arrington, A, Richardson, M A, Marigna, M, Huff, R, Main, M and Newcomb, M D (1992) 'The impact of a parent training program on inner-city African-American families', *Journal of Community Psychology*, 20, 132–47

National Research Council Institute of Medicine (2000) *From Neurons to Neighborhoods: The Science of Early Childhood Development.* Washington: National Academy Press

Nicholson, B, Anderson, M, Fox, R and Brenner, V (2002) 'One Family at a Time: A Prevention Program for At-Risk Parents', *Journal of Counseling and Development*, 80, 362–71

Noblitt, G W, Hare, R D and Noblit, GW (1998) *Meta-Ethnography: Synethesizing Qualitative Studies*. Sage Publications

Norwood, P M, Atkinson, S E, Tellez, K and Saldana, D C (1997) 'Contextualizing Parent Education Programs in Urban Schools: The Impact on Minority Parents and Students', *Urban Education,* 32, 411–32

Office for National Statistics (2002) *National Statistics Online.* Available from: www.statistics.gov.uk, accessed 27/01/03

Offord, M D and Bennett, K J (1994) 'Conduct disorder: long-term outcomes and intervention effectiveness', *Journal of the American Academy of Child and Adolescent Psychiatry,* 33, 1069–78

Ogbu, J U (1981) 'Origins of human competence: a cultural-ecological perspective', *Child Development,* 52, 423–29

Parker-Scott, J (1999) *A study of the impact of a parent education program on recidivism rates of male juveniles* [dissertation]. Pepperdine University

Patterson, G R., DeBaryshe, D and Ramsey, E (1989) 'A Developmental Perspective on Antisocial Behavior', *American Psychologist*, 44, 329–35

Patterson, G, Dishion, T J and Chamberlain, P (1993) 'Outcomes and Methodological Issues Relating to Treatment of Antisocial children' *in* Giles, T R *ed. Handbook of Effective Psychotherapy*. New York: Plenum Press

Patterson, J, Mockford, C, Barlow, J, Pyper, C and Stewart-Brown, S (2002) 'Need and demand for parenting programmes in a general practice setting', *Archives of Disease in Childhood*, 82, 468–71

Pembroke, E (1980) *Parent education as a means of fostering moral development in beginning primary age children* [dissertation]. Loyola University of Chicago

Percy, M S and McIntyre, L (2001) 'Using touchpoints to promote parent self-competence in low-income, minority, pregnant, and parenting teen mothers', *Journal of Pediatric Nursing: Nursing Care of Children and Families*, 16, 180–6

Perez-Nieves, L (2001) *A comparative study of REBT/parent training versus parent training with Hispanic parents of exceptional preschoolers* [dissertation]. St John's University, New York

Pitts, R P (2001) *The effectiveness and acceptability of the modified Effective Black Parenting Program with children exhibiting severe conduct problems* [dissertation]. Lehigh University

Popay, J, Rogers, A and Williams, G (1998) 'Rationale and Standards for the Systematic Review of Qualitative Literature in Health Services Research', *Qualitative Health Research*, 8, 3, 341–51

Pugh, G, De'Ath, E and Smith, C (1994) *Confident Parents, Confident Children: Policy and practice in parent education and support.* National Children's Bureau

Reid, M J, Webster-Stratton, C and Beauchaine, T P (2001) 'Parent training in Head Start: a comparison of program response among African American, Asian American, White, and Hispanic mothers', *Prevention Science*, 2, 209–27

Rowland, S B and Wampler, K S (1983) 'Black and White Mothers' Preferences for Parenting Programs', *Family Relations*, 32, 323–30

Russek, L G and Schwartz, G E (1997a) 'Feelings of parent caring predict health status in midlife: a 35-year follow-up of the Harvard Mastery of Stress Study', *Journal of Behavioural Medicine*, 20, 1–13

Russek, L G and Schwartz, G E (1997b) 'Perceptions of parent caring predict health status in midlife: a 35-year follow-up of the Harvard Mastery of Stress Study', *Psychosocial Medicine,* 59, 144–9

Rutter, M (1996) 'Connections between child and adult psychopathology', *European Journal of Child and Adolescent Psychology*, 5, 4–7

Sandelowski, M, Docherty, S and Emden, C (1997) 'Focus on Qualitative Methods – Qualitative Metasynthesis: Issues and Techniques', *Research in Nursing & Health*, 20, 365–371

Schutt-Aine, I A (1994) *Parenting efficacy and racial identity attitude of African American parents in response to parenting programs with a cultural component* [dissertation]. University of Georgia

Scott, S, Knapp, M, Henderson, J and others (2001a) 'Financial cost of social exclusion: follow up study of antisocial children into adulthood', *British Medical Journal*, 323, 191–4

Scott, S, Spender, Q, Doolan, M, Jacobs, B and Aspland, H (2001b) 'Multi-centre controlled trial of parenting groups for childhood antisocial behaviour in clinical practice', *British Medical Journal*, 323, 194–7

Serketich, W J and Dumas, J E (1996) 'The effectiveness of behavioural parent-training to modify antisocial behaviour in children: a meta analysis', *Behavioural Therapy,* 27, 171–86

Shaffer, J W, Duszynski, K R and Thomas, C B (1982) 'Family attitudes in youth as a possible precursor of cancer among physicians: a search for explanatory mechanisms', *Journal of Behavioural Medicine*, 5, 143–63

Shure, M B and Spivack, G (1978) *Problem Solving Techniques in Childrearing*. California: Jossey-Bass, Inc.

Slaughter, D T (1983) 'Early Intervention and Its Effects on Maternal and Child Development', *Monographs of the Society for Research in Child Development*, 48, 1–92

Smith, C (1996) *Developing Parenting Programmes.* National Children's Bureau

Steele, M, Marigna, M, Tello, J and Johnson, R (2002) *Monograph Parenting Styles and Program Impact (Strengthening Multi-Ethnic Families and Communities: A violence prevention and parent training program)*. Los Angeles, CA: Consulting and Clinical Services

Stewart-Brown, S, Patterson, J, Shaw, R and Morgan, L (2002) *The roots of social capital: A systematic review of longitudinal studies linking relationships in the home in childhood with mental and social health in later life*. Health Services Research Unit, University of Oxford

Stewart-Brown, S, Patterson, J, Mockford, C, Barlow, J, Klimes, I and Pyper, C (in press) 'Impact of a general practice based group parenting programme on the mental health of children and parents 12 months post intervention: quantitative and qualitative results from a controlled trial', *Archives of Disease in Childhood*

Stone, G, McKenry, P and Clark, K (1999) 'Fathers' participation in a divorce education program: a qualitative evaluation', *Journal of Divorce and Remarriage*, 30, 99–113

Strain, P S, Young, C C and Horowitz, J (1981) 'Generalised behavior change during oppositional child training', *Behavior Modification*, 5, 15–26

Taylor, J, Spencer, N and Baldwin, N (2000) 'Social, economic, and political context of parenting', *Archives of Disease in Childhood*, 82, 113–20

Thomas, C B (1976) 'Precursors of premature disease and death. The predictive potential of habits and family attitudes', *Annals of Internal Medicine*, 85, 653–8

Thomas, C B, Duszynski, K R and Shaffer, J W (1979) 'Family attitudes reported in youth as potential predictors of cancer', *Psychosomatic Medicine* 41, 287–302

Thomas, E M (2000) *Parent perceptions of the effective black parenting program* [dissertation]. Walden University, Minneapolis

Todis, B, Irvin, L K, Singer, G H S and Yovanoff, P (1993) 'The self-esteem parent program: Quantitative and qualitative evaluation of a cognitive-behavioral intervention' *in* Singer, G H S and Poers, L E *eds Families, disability and empowerment: Active coping skills and strategies for family interventions.* Baltimore, MD: Paul H Brookes Publishing Co.

Todres, R and Bunston, T (1993) 'Parent-education programme evaluation: a review of the literature', *Canadian Journal of Community Mental Health*, 12, 225–57

Tulloch, E A (1996) *Effectiveness of parent training on perception of parenting skill and reduction of preschool problem behaviors utilizing an ethnically diverse population* [dissertation]. Hofstra University, Hempstead

Villegas, A V (1977) *The efficacy of systematic training for effective parenting with Chicana mothers* [dissertation]. Arizona State University

Webster-Stratton, C and Spitzer, A (1996) 'Parenting a young child with conduct problems: New insights using qualitative methods' *in* Ollendick, T H and Prinz, R J *eds Advances in Clinical Child Psychology*, 18. New York and London: Plenum Press

Webster-Stratton, C, Hollinsworth, T and Kolpacoff, M (1989) 'The long-term effectiveness and clinical significance of three cost-effective training programs for families with conduct-problem children', *Journal of Consulting and Clinical Psychology*, 57, 550–3

Webster-Stratton, C, Kolpacoff, M and Hollinsworth, T (1988) 'Self-administered videotape therapy for families with conduct-problem children: comparison with two cost-effective treatments and a control group', *Journal of Consulting and Clinical Psychology*, 56, 558–66

Wenzlaff, R M and Eisenberg, A R (1998) 'Parent restrictiveness of negative emotions: sowing the seeds of thought suppression', *Psychological Inquiry*, 4, 310–13

Wickrama, K A, Lorenz, F O and Conger, R D (1997) 'Parent support and adolescent physical health status: a latent growth-curve analysis', *Journal of Health and Social Behaviour,* 38, 149–63

Wolfe, R B (1997) *Listening to children: Three studies toward developing, evaluating, and replicating a new approach to parent education, support, and empowerment.* Northwestern University

Ying, Y W (1999) 'Strengthening intergenerational/intercultural ties in migrant families: a new intervention for parents', *Journal of Community Psychology,* 27, 89–96

Yuen, T C (1997) *Filial therapy with immigrant Chinese parents in Canada* [dissertation]. University of North Texas

Appendix 1:
The review: methods and search strategy

Methods

Criteria for including studies in the review

A number of criteria were used to determine whether a study should be included in the review. These criteria were used to guide the search strategy that was developed.

Type of studies/methodology

Studies were included in the review irrespective of the study design/methodology, i.e. both quantitative and qualitative methods.

Types of participants

Only studies evaluating programmes that were specifically directed at parents from minority ethnic groups were included in the review. Minority ethnic parents in this context refers to parents from African, Asian, or Hispanic backgrounds for example, who are living in predominantly British, American or European societies. Programmes in which there is a cultural mix of parents, i.e. studies that have samples that comprise more than 20 per cent white parents, or in which minority ethnic parents represent only a proportion of the entire sample, were excluded from the review. This reflects the fact that it is not possible to reach any conclusions about the specific effects of parenting programmes for minority ethnic parents where a significant proportion of the sample are white.

Types of intervention

The review included evidence concerning both 'traditional' and 'culturally specific' group-based parenting programmes irrespective of the theoretical basis underpinning the programme.

The review included only studies that had evaluated parenting programmes that met the following criteria:

■ Parenting programmes that are delivered on a group basis.
■ Programmes that use a standardised format and can therefore be repeated by others.
■ Programmes which are delivered specifically with the intention of either (i) supporting parents or (ii) improving parenting attitudes/practices, the well-being or relationship of parents and/or children, or family life more generally.

The review excluded studies that evaluated parenting programmes that met the following criteria:

■ Parenting programmes that incorporate other components such as a home visiting component or an intervention that is delivered directly to a child. These studies were excluded because where parenting programmes are combined with other interventions it is not possible to know which part of the intervention was most instrumental in producing change. It would therefore be impossible to reach any conclusions about the effectiveness of the parenting programme in particular.
■ Programmes that are not directed solely at minority ethnic parents.

Types of outcome

The review included studies that evaluated the following types of outcome:

(i) Effectiveness outcomes – this included any measures of the effectiveness of the programme in improving outcomes for parents, children or the family. Both standardised, i.e. those for which there is published evidence of reliability and validity, and non-standardised measures of outcome were included.

(ii) Process outcomes – this included any information concerning the programme and parents' experiences of taking part in it. Information concerning who received the programme, who delivered it, how and in what context, were extracted from the included studies. Data were also extracted concerning parents' experiences of taking part in a parenting programme such as, for example, quotations from in-depth interviews or standardised measures of consumer satisfaction.

Search strategy

A search was undertaken for both published and unpublished studies.

Published studies

The following electronic databases were searched to identify all published studies:

Biomedical sciences databases

Medline Journal Articles (1970 to 2001)

Biological Abstracts Journal Articles (1970 to 2001)

Social Science and General Reference databases

PsychLIT Journal Articles and Chapter/Books (1970 to 2001)

Sociofile; Social Science Citation Index; Health Star Journal Articles (1970 to 2001)

CINAHL (1982 to 2001)

Other sources of information:

The Cochrane Library including CDSR; DARE; and CCT

National Research Register (NRR)

Reference lists of articles identified through database searches and bibliographies of systematic and non-systematic review articles were examined to identify further relevant studies.

Unpublished and ongoing studies

A search was undertaken of Dissertation Abstracts database.
A search was also undertaken of a database maintained by the Race Equality Unit (REU) of UK based parenting programmes for ethnic minority parents.

Search terms

A set of search terms were developed which were optimal for the identification of studies on parenting programmes that are directed at parents from minority ethnic groups. The search terms used were modified to meet the requirements of individual databases as regards differences in fields. No methodological terms were included in order to ensure that all studies, irrespective of methodology, were identified.

Selection of studies

Decisions about which studies to include in the review were undertaken by two independent reviewers. Uncertainties concerning the appropriateness of studies for inclusion in the review were resolved through consultation with a third reviewer. In the case of published studies, this decision was based on titles and abstracts that had been downloaded from the relevant database. All studies were included in the review that met the criteria outlined above.

Quality assessment

Critical appraisal using published criteria was undertaken of both the quantitative and qualitative studies that were included in the review, to provide the reader with the opportunity to assess the reliability of the evidence being summarised.

Data management

Both quantitative and qualitative data were extracted independently by two reviewers using data extraction forms. Where data were not available in either published or unpublished reports, authors were contacted to supply missing information.

Data analysis

Data synthesis – qualitative overview
A narrative synthesis of the findings has been produced. Where available, direct quotations from parents are also provided.

Data synthesis – quantitative overview
The results of individual outcomes from individual studies have been presented and a narrative summary provided with a comprehensive description of the results and what they mean.

Appendix 2: Summary of studies evaluating outcomes for each ethnic group, methodologies and methodological limitations

Black parents

Twenty studies evaluated the effectiveness of parenting programmes with black parents and children. Four of these studies were randomised controlled trials. A number of parent and child outcomes were measured including emotional and behavioural adjustment, self-concept, moral reasoning, play, parent attitudes and behaviour, and parents' stress. The four RCTs evaluated three traditional/translated parenting programmes (Incredible Years Programme; PET; Mothers' Discussion Programme) (Reid, Webster-Stratton and Beauchaine, 2001; Pembroke, 1980; Slaughter, 1983) and one culturally specific programme (EBPP) (Pitts, 2001).

Eleven controlled studies were included evaluating a range of parenting programmes. Seven studies evaluated the effectiveness of traditional parenting programmes (Booker, 1986; Creswell-Betsch, 1979; Gordon-Rosen and Rosen, 1984; Levant and Slattery, 1982; Levant and Slobodian, 1981; Shure and Spivack, 1978; Wolfe, 1997). Programmes included ICPSS (Shure and Spivack, 1978), an Adlerian programme (Gordan-Rosen, 1982), Listening to Children (Wolfe, 1997) and several unnamed programmes. Two studies evaluated culturally adapted programmes – STEP (Alvy, 1988) and Independent Life Skills Preparation and Communication Interaction Programmes (Carten, 1986) and three evaluated culturally specific programmes (Norwood and others, 1997; Myers and others, 1992 (two studies)) including the EBPP (Myers and others, 1992). Two comparative studies were undertaken. One study compared the effectiveness of a culturally adapted (PTB) and culturally specific programme (EBPP) (Schutt-Aine, 1994) and one study compared the impact of a culturally specific (PRAISE) and traditional parenting programme (PDFY) (Moore, 1992) with a control group. One-group designs were used to evaluate the traditional 'Listening to Children' Programme (Wolfe, 1997) and the culturally specific parenting SMFC programme (Steele and others, 2002). One retrospective study did not specify the type of parenting programme being evaluated (Parker-Scott, 1999).

None of the controlled or one-group designs undertook the random allocation of families to either intervention or control group. In the absence of randomisation, it is important that families in the intervention group are either matched with families in the control group to reduce the influence of important confounding variables such as social class or education, etc., or that any differences at baseline in confounding variables are controlled for in the analysis. No matching was undertaken in any of these studies (i.e. they all utilised a non-equivalent control group), and only two studies undertook an adjusted analysis controlling for baseline differences (Norwood and others, 1997; Gordon-Rosen and Rosen, 1984). This means that eight studies report findings in which no matching was undertaken, and no adjustment for confounding (Alvy, 1988; Booker, 1986; Carten, 1986; Creswell-Betsch, 1979; Levant and Slattery, 1982; Levant and Slobodian, 1981; Moore, 1992; Myers and others, 1992 (two studies); Schutt-Aine, 1994; Shure and Spivack, 1978). One further study also failed to provide baseline data (i.e. the post-intervention scores were compared) (Wolfe, 1997). One study was undertaken retrospectively (Parker-Scott, 1999).

Hispanic parents

Eight studies evaluated the effectiveness of a parenting programme in improving outcomes for Hispanic parents and their children. Four studies used randomised controlled trials to evaluate the effectiveness of a translated Incredible Years programme (Reid, Webster-Stratton and Beauchaine, 2001), two culturally adapted Adlerian programmes (Davis, 1994; Villegas, 1977) and a traditional REBT programme (Perez Nieves, 2001) in improving a range of parent and child outcomes for Hispanic parents including emotional and behavioural adjustment, school achievement, parent behaviour, parent attitudes, parent mental health, and use of community services. Two studies used controlled designs to evaluate the effectiveness of a translated Exploring Parenting Curriculum (Copeland, 1981) and a series of translated (unnamed) parenting programmes (Leal, 1985) in improving a range of outcomes for Hispanic parents including parent attitudes, knowledge of child development, and social support. Neither of these studies reported on any child outcomes. In addition, the Leal (1985) study did not undertake random allocation to groups or matching, and undertook an analysis of the post-test results only without any adjustment for pre-test differences or confounders (i.e. did not compare the change in both groups). One study utilised a one-group design to evaluate the effectiveness of the culturally specific SMFC programme in improving both child and parent outcomes (Steele and others, 2002). A range of outcomes were measured including emotional and behavioural adjustment, self-esteem, anxiety, delinquency, racial identity, parent–child interaction, stress, and parenting attitudes and behaviour. One study comprised a retrospective evaluation (Parker-Scott, 1999). This study evaluated the effectiveness of a number of traditional parenting programmes (not named) that were run to help families with troubled youth.

Asian (Chinese-American parents/Asian Pacific Islanders)

Five studies evaluated the effectiveness of a parenting programme in improving outcomes for Asian (Chinese-American or Asian Pacific Islanders) parents and children. Three studies were randomised controlled trials (Chau and Landreth, 1997; Reid, Webster-Stratton and Beauchaine, 2001; Yuen, 1997) and two were one-group designs (Steele and others, 2002; Ying, 1999). Two of the three randomised controlled trials evaluated the effectiveness of translated filial therapy parenting programmes in improving a range of parent and child outcomes (Chau and Landreth, 1997; Yuen, 1997), and the remaining RCT evaluated the effectiveness of the translated Webster-Stratton Incredible Years Programme. It should be noted that the Chau and Landreth (1997) study was a quasi-randomised controlled trial in which parents were allocated to groups on the basis of availability. This may therefore have introduced bias into the design. The remaining studies (Steele and others, 2002; Ying, 1999) evaluated culturally specific programmes.

There was also evidence of improved parenting attitudes and behaviour, parent mental health, and parent–child interaction. Positive results were also obtained from the two one-group design studies of culturally specific programmes.

Native Americans

Two studies evaluated the effectiveness of a parenting programme in improving outcomes for Native American parents and children. One evaluated the effectiveness of a translated parenting programme using a controlled study (Glover and Landreth, 2000) and the second evaluated the effectiveness of a culturally specific parenting programme using a one-group design (Steele and others, 2002).

Ethnically mixed groups

Four studies evaluated the effectiveness of parenting programmes in improving outcomes for mixed ethnic groups (these studies included parents from a range of ethnic groups including Asian, Hispanic, African-American, Mexican-American, white, etc.). One evaluated the effectiveness of a traditional programme (STAR) using a randomised controlled trial (Nicholson and others, 2002). A second evaluated the effectiveness of a culturally specific programme (SOS) using a controlled design (Tulloch, 1996) and two further studies evaluated the effectiveness of unnamed traditional programmes using one-group designs (Mendez-Baldwin, 2001; Percy and McIntyre, 2001).